THE KE...
WORLI...

Pyramids have been found throughout the world, in places as far apart as Egypt, China, Peru, Mexico, and even in the middle of the United States! Who built these mysterious structures, and why?

Martin Ebon has gathered the experts and put all the evidence, information, and experimentation into one book, starting with studies on the pyramids of the ancients; moving on to the psychic powers of the pyramids; exploring the use of pyramidal shapes in preserving organic materials, and sharpening blades; and explaining how to build your own functional pyramid. It's all here in this fascinating collection of articles about the world beyond our five senses, the puzzling psychic energies that we call . . .

MYSTERIOUS PYRAMID POWER

MYSTERIOUS PYRAMID POWER

EDITED BY
MARTIN EBON

A SIGNET BOOK

NEW AMERICAN LIBRARY

ACKNOWLEDGMENTS

"The Pharaoh's Curse," by Gordon Thistlewait, originally appeared under the title "The Riddle of the Pharaoh's Curse" in Occult, January, 1976. Copyright © 1976 by CBS Publications, the Consumer Publishing Division of CBS, Inc.

"Literature of the Great Pyramid," by Martin Gardner, originally appeared as a chapter, "The Great Pyramid," in Fads and Fallacies in the Name of Science, published 1957 by Dover Publications, a revised and expanded edition of the work originally published by G. P. Putnam's Sons, 1952, under the title, In the Name of Science. Copyright © 1952 by Martin Gardner. Copyright © 1957 by Martin Gardner. Reprinted by permission.

"Discussions in Moscow," by Benson Herbert, originally appeared as part of a more extensive report in The International Journal of Paraphysics, Vol. 6, No. 5. Copyright © 1974 by Paraphysical Laboratory, Downton, Wiltshire, U.K. Reprinted by permission.

"How Much Would It Cost to Build the Great Pyramid," by Russ Martin, originally appeared under the title "Building the Great Pyramid" in TWA Ambassador, July, 1973. Copyright © 1973 by Trans World Airlines. Reprinted by permission.

"Pyramids, Magnetism, and Gravity," by Alexander Ross, originally appeared under the title "A Pyramid that Sharpens Razor Blades" in En Route, Air Canada's inflight magazine, February, 1973. Copyright © 1973 by Air Canada. Reprinted by permission.

"An Oraccu Is Not a Pyramid—Or Is It?" by Serge V. King, originally appeared under the title "Experimenting with Pyramid Power" in Probe the Unknown, October, 1973. Copyright © 1973 by Rainbow Publications, Inc. Reprinted by permission.

"Pyramids Around the World," by Warren Smith, originally appeared under the title "Mysterious Pyramids Around the World" in Saga, October, 1973. Copyright © 1973 by Gambi Publications, Inc. Reprinted by permission.

Contents

It All Began
on the French Riviera

A twelve-year-old boy, Hubert Larcher, was walking through the streets of Nice, in southern France, back in 1932, when his attention was attracted by an odd window display: a miniature pyramid, under which were placed the dried-up bodies of several small animals. The boy eventually, became one of Europe's leading parapsychologists, as well as consulting physician to the French Ministry of Justice. Today, Dr. Larcher is a member of the governing committee of the Institut Métapsychique International in Paris and editor of its journal, the *Revue Métapsychique*.

The unusual display the little boy had seen in a side street of the Mediterranean city, hub of the French Riviera, had been arranged in the show window of the Quincaillerie, Bovis & Passeron (a *quincaillerie* is roughly the equivalent of a hardware store). One of the co-owners of the store, Antoine Bovis, was a man of inventive mind and skill. He had built the miniature pyramid because he was convinced that a model proportioned after the Pyramid of Cheops would create a mysterious condition, which, among other things, would counteract decomposition and thus encourage the mummification of animal bodies. Mr. Bovis's personal study of these phenomena was based on the use of his patented pendulum.

Among the items young Hubert saw in Bovis's show window were instruments used to measure the impact of radiesthesia, the elusive qualities he believed to have isolated in experiments with pyramids and other shapes. Bovis attributed different qualities to the interiors of squares, pipes, funnels, and other shapes. He lectured and wrote about his ideas, saying that he had visited the Cheops Pyramid. There, Bovis said, he had measured the interior radiesthesic qualities of the King's Chamber, which he found to be identical to those in the pyramid models he constructed using proportionately the same dimensions.

1

Today's worldwide fascination with pyramid shapes and powers is the direct result of the determination of the eccentric Mr. Bovis, whose specially designed "Bovis Special Magnetic Pendulum" was used in numerous experiments and led its inventor to claim he had developed a physical "Law of Radiesthesia Action." In addition to his Nice hardware shop, Bovis also operated a firm, "Artisanat A. Bovis," which constructed his "paradiamagnetic" pendulum and various magnetic devices designed to aid mummification.

The Nice artisan's claims attracted the attention of a radio technician in Czechoslovakia, Dr. Karel Drbal. At first, he was skeptical of the hardware store owner's claims. But, having read Bovis's reports, he began a correspondence with him, and soon the letters moving from Nice to Prague enabled the Czech engineer to build models after the Cheops pattern. Lo and behold: they worked! Drbal writes in Max Toth's book *Pyramid Power*, that to his great astonishment, "I, like Mr. Bovis, was able to create mummifications" of "beef, calf or lamb meat, eggs, flowers and even dead reptiles such as frogs, snakes, lizards, etc." Drbal had an "agreeable correspondence" with Bovis, although he struck Drbal as a little "too magic" for the standards of a radio technician. "He claimed," Drbal says, "to find with his pendulum radiations in everything he touched."

Soon, Drbal, the disciple, was outdoing his master in publishing reports on pyramid experiments in French and Belgian journals. He felt that "some energy" must be present inside pyramids, and this led him to experiments with razor blades. He expected this force to blunt his Blue Gillette. But the very opposite happened. Instead of being able to shave only about five times with each blade, Drbal found he could shave fifty times in comfort with those blades he had placed inside the pyramid.

The thousands of close shaves Drbal had during a quarter of a century varied sufficiently in quality to cause him to believe that inside the pyramid the edge of a blade becomes a "living entity" whose quality fluctuates. He might get a poor shave one day, but the edge could recover and give him an excellent shave the very next day. This prompted the Czech engineer to think in very practical terms. Perhaps, he wondered, there was a market for a device that could keep a razor blade sharp for months; at that time, blades were expensive and in short supply.

In 1949, Drbal applied to the Patent Examination Commission of Czechoslovakia, thinking it might take the commission two to three years to examine and approve the Razor Blade Pyramid. But ten years passed before he received Patent No. 91304. During this time, the engineer had to develop a hypothesis as to how the device actually worked. He theorized that it might operate by "energization of the resonant cavity" of the model pyramids by means of cosmic microwaves, mainly from the sun, with "help from the concentrating earth magnetic field." With the pyramid finally patented, Dr. Drbal was able to distribute cardboard models and continue his research on the firmer basis of official recognition.

Although the Czech engineer wrote for a variety of publications in eastern and western Europe, describing his experiments and results, worldwide attention did not come until the visit of two American writers, Sheila Ostrander and Lynn Schroeder. As narrated in their book, *Psychic Discoveries Behind the Iron Curtain*, they saw one of Drbal's little pyramids in the Prague home of a friend. It was sitting on top of a bookcase, a razor blade inside and balanced on top of a matchbox. They were intrigued. The story of Bovis's pilgrimage to the Cheops Pyramid, as told them by a Czech friend, had the Frenchman stopping in the King's Chamber, "tired with the heat." He found the air unusually humid and was startled by "garbage cans in the chamber containing cats and other animals that had wandered into the pyramid, lost their way, and died."

Ostrander and Schroeder, reconstructing Bovis's thoughts, assumed that he might have said, "There's something strange about those animals. There's no smell of decay from them." They were "dehydrated, *mummified*, despite the humidity." The two writers met Dr. Drbal and heard of his invention, his youth in Vienna, his seven years in Paris, his piano playing and active investigation of parapsychological phenomena. They quoted him as suggesting that "just as the special shape of a violin gives tone and quality to a bow touching a string, the special shape of a pyramid apparently is a resonant cavity for the 'live' crystals of a razor blade."

Drbal toyed with related ideas. Why were witches pictured wearing conical hats? He had made hats in the shape of a pyramid, and people had said they relieved headaches. Drbal treated the matter lightly. It might be necessary to custom-make such hats, and maybe even get a patent on his "Magic Hat." Schroeder and Ostrander asked themselves, "Does the pyramid have other uses besides food preservation and razor sharpening? Could it speed the growth of plants, purify water? Does energy of the pyramid have anything to do with psychic force?" Their answer: "We don't know yet." But since their book appeared several years ago, others have tried to answer these and a good many other questions—and that's what this book is about: pyramid power, as it has become part of today's scene in America.

The pyramids of Egypt, notably the so-called Cheops Pyramid, are impressive and mysterious enough in their own right, as the firsthand reports by Professor Brier and the Reverend Kinnear—at the beginning of this volume—clearly indicate. The architectural and spiritual impact of the pyramids remains strong to this day, and their actual usage, means of construction, and religio-historical aspect are still sufficiently elusive to have fascinated generations, past and present. Right now, the pyramids themselves and pyramid-shapes generally have become the focus of a wide assortment of experiments and cults. The New Horizons Research Foundation of Toronto undertook carefully controlled laboratory experiments to test the razor blade phenomena. Mrs. Iris Owen, who reports on this work, notes that claims made for the benefits from pyramids now include just about everything from improved meditation to sleep and child growth.

Quite simply, pyramids now embody any number of religious and secular concepts, symbols, and hopes. In the nineteenth century, and even in our day, much has been made of the alleged mathematical aspects of the pyramids that make them into coded vessels of biblical prophecy. The literature of this search is surveyed by Mr. Gardner in his contribution to this volume. But this mathematician-satirist also is responsible for one of the most amusing hoaxes in the pyramid field to appear in the field of pure pyramidology. Gardner, whom *Time* (April 2, 1975) called "The Mathemagician," publishes a monthly "Mathematical Games" column in *Scientific American.* Usually, readers find his column a repository of intriguing mathematical puzzles, concepts, and challenges. But in the June, 1974, issue of the magazine, they encountered an apparent narrative of the author's journey to Pyramid Lake, Nevada (there really is such a place, the article had a photograph of Pyramid Rock in the lake), where he visited with Dr. Irving Joshua Matrix, "renowned numerologist," his beautiful, dark-haired, half-Japanese daughter, Iva; he also met Matrix's Paiute Indian servant, Ree, who had "only a single front tooth," so everyone called him, "One-Tooth Ree." (Are you beginning to catch on? "One-Tooth-Ree" can be read as One, Two, Three!)

The article includes an arcane numerological conversation Gardner allegedly had with his old and obviously imaginary friend Dr. Matrix. They visited his factory, where twenty Indians assembled six-inch pyramid models in one wing, while a smaller group cut and packaged the unassembled models in another wing. Matrix talks about "psi-org energy," which the Egyptians used to "float heavy stones across the desert when they built their pyramids." The good doctor assured his visitor that one Dr. Harold Puton had made "hundreds of carefully controlled tests" showing that inside a pyramid "one is more telepathic, more clairvoyant, more precognitive." The author asked "about the pyramid's power to prevent and even reverse decay of organic matter," and was told Dr. Matrix had "applied for numerous patents that exploited this aspect of psi-org: a pyramid refrigerator and freezer, a pyramid coffin (no embalming necessary), a pyramid septic tank."

And so it went. Until the end of the article, where Gardner reports that Dr. Matrix had been indicted by the State of Nevada for selling pyramid franchises to people who in turn sold franchises to others, "a typical pyramid scheme of the sort that sooner or later was bound to collapse." He concluded with the report that Dr. Matrix and his daughter had "entered one of their large pyramids and teleported themselves to a monastery in Tibet."

This last bit of business, the teleporting to Tibet, should have alerted the sophisticated readers of *Scientific American* that they were being April-Fooled, were being had, and were having their legs pulled, all in one fell swoop. But no. Gardner, who can be tart and tough when it comes to judging the gullibility of mankind, was confirmed in his skepticism when he received hundreds of letters asking for more information on "psi-org energy," a term he had simply made up. A reader from Hawaii wrote that Gardner's column had "really turned people on" in his area: one woman had moved into a glass-and-plastic pyramid beside a jungle stream, and a health food store was keeping its produce under a giant pyramid. In fact, the Hawaiian group was ready to pay Gardner to come and lecture about the new pyramid discoveries. As he recounts in a "Postscript" to the original column in his anthology *The Incredible Dr. Matrix,* Martin

Gardner was even more startled when he received a letter from a New York publisher, who offered him an advance of $15,000 for a book on pyramid power. Gardner wondered whether the man was serious, and so he went to have lunch with him. The publisher was, indeed, quite serious. He had taken the meticulously written satire for the Real McCoy. Quick to recover his poise, he suggested that Gardner write the book under a pseudonym and then "expose the book later as a hoax, provided he had a full year to promote it as a serious study." Gardner declined.

Satire, obviously, is insufficient to curb man's unconscious desire to capture magical powers associated with ancient traditions and forces or entities outside earthly existence. As a result, the pyramids are focal points for a veritable jungle of hypotheses. Aside from their mathematical-prophetical qualities, pyramids are associated with many and sometimes contradictory concepts. Warren Smith, whose overview of worldwide pyramids appears in this volume, listed several hypotheses in his book *The Secret Forces of the Pyramids.* They included the idea that pyramids are "our link with the stars," suggesting that "alien spacemen from other worlds built the Great Pyramid of Gizeh as a coded message of their visitation during ancient times." Further, the Great Pyramid might be "a model of our Universe," somehow providing open "routes" for Unidentified Flying Objects (UFOs) through a "triangular universe." Also, pyramids have been described as a possible "library of ancient knowledge," whereby the Cheops Pyramid "could contain up to 3,700 of these secret depositories." Smith notes that there has been speculation that pyramids provide a "clue to the lost continent or Atlantis," hidden within "those gigantic piles of stone on the Gizeh plateau and elsewhere in the world." And the pyramids could be "a key to lost energy." This ties in with the Bovis Drbal hypothesis of power within the pyramidal "cavity." Smith also picks up the idea that pyramids were left behind by entities from outer space, who had visited and left the earth; assuming this, the pyramids might be these space men's means for "monitoring the earth."

There is a widespread tendency to associate one mysterious fact or event with others that are similarly unexplained. The result can be one grand House of Cards of assorted data held together by little more than personal preference and interest. Take, for example, the idea of linking pyramids and reincarnation; I am picking this concept simply because i hasn't been dramatized in recent literature. But I am encouraged to do so by the writings of several reincarnation authorities, notably the author and psychic Ruth Montgomery. In her book *Companions Along the Way*, Mrs. Montgomery states that spirits told her that 2,000 years ago she had been a girl, also named Ruth, the third sister of the biblical Lazarus. Communicating by automatic writing, they said, "As a little girl of seven you saw the bright star and the shepherds who assembled in the village square and when you heard reports that the star heralded the birth of a babe in Bethlehem, your excitement knew no bounds." In her book, Mrs. Montgomery tells us that her other incarnations included three previous lives in Ancient Egypt. In an earlier book, *A World Beyond*, she reported that prominent personalities of the past have been reincarnated and are now active among us; specifically, she mentioned that President Abraham Lincoln "has returned in the flesh after a rather long period" and "now lives in New Orleans, where he is studying the Southern race problem in all its manifest facets." Lincoln's reincarnated personality is identified by Mrs. Montgomery as "an adult" who "works with universities and foundations to find proper solutions."

If Mrs. Montgomery can have lived in Ancient Egypt and Lincoln is now among us as an expert in race relations, might it not be possible that men and women associated with creation of the Pyramid of Cheops have also been reincarnated and are perhaps even now contributing to a solution of the pyramid enigma? If one advances this point a step further, one quickly comes across a dramatic hypothesis advanced by some reincarnationists: that the early ability of child prodigies is due to the fact that they carry over from a previous incarnation the very talents that surface so early in their current lives. One French authority, Professor Robert Tocquet, has suggested that men of the *Wunderkind* type, such as the composer Wolfgang Amadeus Mozart, might have matured in an early incarnation and came into their future existence with their talents fully developed. As it happens, the American pyramid scene has at least one man whose credentials place him in the prodigy category: Pat G. Flanagan of Glendale, California. We learn from the *Houston Chronicle* (November 17, 1975) that Flanagan received "a measure of renown" at age seventeen by developing "the neurophone, a device intended to enable some deaf people to hear." It took him several years to obtain a patent for this device,

Flanagan told the Texas paper, and he "sold it to a company in New York in 1963." Flanagan was mentioned in *Life* magazine (September 14, 1962) among the "Most Important Young Men and Women in the U.S." Tom Valentine, in *The Great Pyramid*, refers to the former prodigy as having been "acknowledged as a genius by many scientists who have worked for him."

Pat Flanagan has published several books, beginning with *Pyramid Power*, which lists his many projects: "The pyramids were made of various materials including cardboard, wood, plaster, plexiglas, steel, copper, aluminum, cement and combinations of the above materials . . . In the duplication of Bovis's experiments, many perishable food items were tried in the pyramids of various shapes and sizes, of different materials, and different orientations, and in different locations in the pyramid itself. . . . My contribution to the field of food mummification is in the discovery that the pyramid will preserve food in any part of the structure, as well as in the King's Chamber as reported by Bovis."

Flanagan's research included shaving over 200 times with a blade "treated in the pyramid." But he shaved the same number of times with another blade by "rinsing my razor out in pure de-ionized distilled water after every shave." He developed a number of devices, including a "psychotronic twirler." In 1974, Flanagan went to Egypt, where he "culminated years of research into unusual energies by spending the night in the King's Chamber of the Pyramid of Cheops." There, he "made contact with a powerful force" that changed his life "in drastic ways." He discontinued his association with a company that manufactured pyramids; he found a number of shapes "more efficient than the pyramid."

Pat Flanagan states in a later book, *Beyond Pyramid Power*, that pyramid energy "has been taken from the realm of the mystical toy, and projected into the infancy of a new technology that could literally change the living conditions of man on this planet," including voice communication, propulsion, and treatment of seeds and of water. Summarizing the "unusual effects on organic media" ascribed to pyramid power, Flanagan stated that they were "found to mummify meat and other foods without decay; improve the flavor of foods and cigarettes; age wine and other drinks; increase the life span of small animals, improve the growth rate of plants; improve and enhance the meditative state; and keep razor blades from becoming dull!" The author established the Flanagan Research Foundation.

Toth in New York and Flanagan in California may be said to represent the east-west axis of pyramidology in the United States. There are, however, many others throughout the country who have experimented with pyramids privately or commercially. Among them is Mankind Research Unlimited in Washington, D.C., directed by Dr. Carl Schleicher, who says that his findings will have "far-reaching impact on virtually every area of human life." Schleicher believes that pyramid studies point to "the need for radical changes in the way we grow and package food and design our homes and cities." His views are supported by a Washington physician, Dr. Brosi Vern, who regards the pyramid work as "a breakthrough in both the physical and biological sciences."

Dr. Schleicher told the *National Enquirer* (September 23, 1975) that his group had placed black-eyed peas and limabean seeds under a pyramid, under a cube-shaped structure, and in an open space. They were not watered. He reported that the peas under the pyramid "grew at 1.5 times the speed of the uncovered seeds and 1.129 times as fast as those under the cube." Hamburger meat placed under a pyramid decayed at about half the rate of chopped meat kept under the cube or in the open. The temperature in this experiment was kept at a level of 70 degrees.

The Mankind Research Unlimited group also claims that six volunteers who slept under a pyramid for four nights reported sleeping "better," which was "verified by electronic monitors that measure stress." The report said their blood pressure "dropped more than usual after ordinary sleep." The magazine communicated these findings to Dr. Drbal and quoted the originator of the razor blade process as saying that some of his own research "especially in the area of plant growth," coincides with the results of Schleicher's work and that he was "especially intrigued by his findings on the relationship between sleep and the pyramid form."

Elsewhere in this volume, in the chapter contributed by Wanda Sue Childress, experiments in other parts of the country, notably Arizona and California, are reported in considerable number. The Toth, Flanagan, and Schleicher efforts are only part of a nationwide pattern. Nevertheless, controlled and repeated laboratory testing would still seem to be required to replicate these experiments and results. Experiments on a much larger scale, undertaken by balanced teams rather than by a few individuals, will be necessary to produce data statistically broad enough to achieve acceptance in scientific circles.

When one speculates on the possible relationship between pyramids and the reincarnation doctrine, one must allow for the role which the late Edgar Cayce, often called the "Seer of Virginia Beach," has played in perpetuating both mystiques. Mr. Cayce went into sleeplike states, akin to trances, during which he seemed to communicate data from an invisible bank of knowledge. Many people received "readings" from Cayce that told of their previous lives, often in Ancient Egypt. His "readings" have been numbered in the archives of the Association for Research and Enlightenment at Virginia Beach. In reading No. 249-151, Cayce said that during "the laying of the pyramid and the building of same," forces were used that "made for the activity of bringing them from those very mountains where there had been those places of refuge." As to how the building materials were transported, a question that has baffled analysts for centuries, Cayce reading No. 5748-6 alleged that this was done by some form of energy akin to psychokinesis (mind over matter), utilizing "those forces of nature as make for iron to swim," while "stone floats in the air in the same manner."

The idea that the pyramids are, in some esoteric way, storehouses of knowledge, was also reflected in Cayce readings. He said that Atlanteans, people from the legendary sunken continent of Atlantis, helped to build the pyramids. Reading No. 281-43 stated that "the Atlanteans aided in their activities with the creating of that called Pyramid, with its records of events of the earth through its activity in all of the ages to that in which the new dispensation is to come." One such reading, No. 1011-1, suggested the presence of someone who had been involved in the construction of the Great Pyramid; it said that "the entity was then among the *builders* of the period." Cayce's readings were often elusive, and the word "entity" might have referred to a discarnate spirit communicating through him, to Cayce himself, or to someone present in the flesh. This reading also stated that disputes "arose through those periods of activities, as to what pertained to or was in keeping with the astrological aspects, the numerological aspects, and those things that would be the more lasting in their [the pyramids] relationships to the climatic conditions, the atmospheric pressures and the various influences had upon those temples and those monoliths."

Clearly, the pyramids have been and are now a focal point for a mixture of imaginative concepts that have only been tested on a relatively limited scale. Beginning with Bovis and continuing with Drbal and his imitators, hundreds of individuals and small groups have experimented with pyramids and, more recently, with a variety of other physical shapes. In each case, the search has been designed to locate and utilize a form of energy that cannot be measured in electronic terms; Bovis's pendulum has not survived. During the Second International Congress on Psychotronic Research, held in Monte Carlo from June 30 to July 4, 1975, Drbal paid tribute to French researchers who, he suggested, were opening "new horizons on relationships between matter and shape." The whole question of the emanation of certain as yet uncharted energies from inanimate objects, vegetable and animal matter is open to further research. This cuts into the territory of psychosomatic medicine, particularly into the apparent ability of some persons to communicate healing powers through their hands or in other ways.

It seemed to me that the people who put pyramid power on the map should have the final word in this introduction to the subject. I therefore asked Karel Drbal, the Czech engineer who turned the ideas of M. Bovis into his "razor blade pyramid," just where he stands on the matter right now. At the age of seventy-two, Drbal is something like an "Elder Statesman of Pyramidology." He no longer writes on the subject, but reports that on April 7, 1976, he shaved with the same blade for the eighty-first time; it was a Czechoslovak-made "Astra" blade. He had just read an article by a Soviet scientist, Professor Bakirov, published in the journal of the University of Tomsk, Western Siberia, *Za Sovetsku Vedu* (May 29, 1975), called "Is It Still a Riddle? Visits with Interesting People," who reported on talks with Drbal and others in Prague and on his own positive experiences with the "razor blade pyramid."

Looking back to 1949, Drbal says: "I have used only 80 razor blades during this whole period; getting 100 shaves was no rarity. When one calculates that only 80 razor blades were used during 27 years and allows that 27 times 365 days amounts to 9,855 days, we arrive at an average of approximately 123 shaves per blade. This means that my blades aren't psychic, but have had a purely physical function!"

Commenting on the inspiration which Bovis' work had on his own studies, Drbal views the Frenchman as something of a "white magician." As he sees him in retrospect, Bovis "was anything but a physicist and his concept of a 'magnetic chamber' in the Cheops Pyramid must be regarded as an exclusively radiesthesic definition, and not as in the realm of physics." Drbal says this today about Bovis: "He was purely a radiesthesic-oriented researcher, a man of the psychic—or, in modern terms, a 'psi man.'" The Greek letter *Psi* is commonly used among parapsychologists to indicate the psychic factor; in this sense, Bovis would have been psychically gifted—his findings based on extrasensory or intuitive gifts rather than on strictly scientific principles. Despite the difference between the approaches of the two men, Drbal recalls that Bovis's writings "led to my own precise biophysical experiments with pyramid models and thus to my paper on the razor blade pryamid.'"

Drbal says today that he "wanted to free myself from the 'Cheops Mystery,' as I am not a mystic, but a microwave technician, radio engineer, and physicist. It is for this reason that I searched for another, more appropriate form, outside the cocoon of the mysterious." For this reason, he constructed a pyramid, "much lower than the Cheops Pyramid," which he called the "Euler Pyramid" after the Swiss mathematician and physicist, Leonhard Euler. The construction's height was established with the mathematical formula $h \times e = a$; in this calculation, a is the base line of the basic square; e stands for Euler's "irrational number of 2.71828+, or about 2.72. Drbal says, "When I selected a height of 5 centimeters, the size of my best razor blade pyramid, the proportions became $5 \times 2.72 = 13.6$ centimeters, or, roughly 13.5 centimeters. The pyramid is designed with the borders of the square north-to-south; the same goes for the razor blade, which is placed on a cork base that is one third the height at the bottom, approximately 1.65 centimeters in height, also placed on a north-south axis. I arrived at the 'Euler Type' by way of numerous empirical tests. This is no secret method—one simply has to define the measurements along these lines." Drbal says that "this carton pyramid is also quite excellent for mummifications, at about 20 centimeters in height, at which point a is equivalent to $20 \times 2.718 = 54.36$, or about 55 centimeters long." He adds that "such pyramids achieve mummification over a period of two weeks, including steaks weighing 100 grams."

The Czech engineer remains open-minded toward the extensive tests and writings undertaken by the radiesthesists, notably Count A. de Belizal, Dr. Albert Leprince, Georges Lakhovsky, Henri Mager, and others. He regards his task as that of a researcher who seeks "pearls in the sand" of their works; he believes that the experiments of these men should be reexamined by physicists, chemists, and biologists, and should not be dismissed out of hand. Drbal looks askance at the "full bloom" of exotic experiments with pyramids. He is dubious about such procedures as "using the dangerous minus zone on the lower level of a pyramid tent for meditation." He says: "I do not wish to pass *a priori* judgment on such experiments, but meditation, long-distance effects of pyramid power, and other tests of this sort are outside my own concepts." He adds, "Despite my advanced years I'd rather spend my time with exact experiments with Belizal's radiation, notably its not only biological but also physical impact on such things as colloids, or on certain macro-molecules."

Speaking of his personal life, the "Father of the Razor Blade Pyramid" says he finds the best physical and mental relaxation with "really good music, a truly fine book, and the beauty of nature." Drbal's personal delight is mountain climbing. For some eighteen years, he made yearly excursions into his homeland's stunning Tatra Mountains. He says that such climbs, some of them lasting as long as ten hours, "are preferable to mystical aspirations." My "magic" life, he concludes, is "in Work, Art and Nature."

Having noted Drbal's personal appraisal of the status of pyramidology today, what about Lynn Schroeder and Sheila Ostrander, the Dynamic Duo who brought his research to the attention of the Western countries, notably the United States? Now that pyramid experiments have taken off in all directions, they confess to feeling at times "like Mickey Mouse as the Sorcerer's Apprentice." This suggests that they have seen Walt Disney's *Fantasia*, in which Mickey acts out the traditional fairy-tale apprentice who is overwhelmed when everything around him, such as brooms, multiplies into threatening armies. Schroeder and Ostrander say that this feeling overcomes them "particularly when photos arrive showing elderly doctor so-and-so with a pyramid on his head," with a caption saying that "he has been wearing the pyramid for three weeks, and we'll all be interested in hearing what he says when he speaks." They don't mention the alternate possibilities that the pyramid shape, according to research so far, might either sharpen or mummify the good doctor's brain! Seriously, Ostrander and Schroeder are most interested in the potential use of pyramids in improving agriculture. They have heard that the Royal Ontario Horticulture Society had "good success with wire pyramids." An "intriguing project," they report, is going on outside Toronto, where a retired decorator, Mr. Les Brown, is now devoting his energies and funds "to do farming with pyramids," using a three-level prototype model thirty feet high. Eventually, Brown wants to use pyramids that are sixty-four feet high.

Schroeder and Ostrander find Brown "genuinely concerned with world starvation and the rising cost of food." He told them he had achieved "tremendous growth in productivity," whereby tomato vines that usually produced ten to fourteen pounds yielded between fifty and sixty pounds in the pyramid. Beyond this, Brown hopes for six growing seasons per year, even in cold Ontario, Canada. Lynn Schroeder says: "One thing he did struck me. He put a raw egg on a pyramid generator and left it open to the air for three weeks, until it resembled a plastic model. Then he added water to reconstitute it, poached the egg, and said it tasted fine and fresh. He's working on the thesis that mummified food can be kept almost indefinitely without losing nutritive value. Lovely, if so . . ."

In Toronto, the *Financial Post Magazine* (April, 1976) reported that "the University of Guelph, one of Canada's most respected agricultural schools, is doing experiments with pyramids." However, the article, by Wayne Lilley, entitled "The Pyramid Pushers," reported "no response difference between plants growing inside or outside pyramids." The author quoted Dr. Ib Nonnecke, chairman of the university's horticultural department, as saying that "both experimental and control groups of plants proved subject to the same insects and disease and there was no difference in growth rate." A second set of pyramid experiments, undertaken in February, 1976, confirmed the earlier tests; Professor Herman Tiessen stated that "pyramids have no effect at all on the growth of plants" and that he regretted "any credibility that the university experiments might have lent to the movement of pyramid power."

Ostrander and Schroeder, looking back on the trend they started, now both think "there is some sort of energy phenomena, but suspect we are still in the Leyden jar and kite-flying stage as far as using this like any other form of energy. [The Leyden jar, developed at the University of Leyden, Holland, in the eighteenth century, was the earliest form of electrical condenser; the kite was a forerunner of the lightning rod.] We like the agricultural uses and wish more people would try this approach because it's practical, can help the world and give visible, objective results. Also, if this does work, it would help to bring in the larger interest needed for full-scale research on a new form of energy."

Schroeder and Ostrander are also intrigued by the underlying mass psychology elements that have made pyramid study so popular. People seem attracted to the pyramid shape as if it were part of a "collective unconscious movement." This fascination suggests that the pyramid may be an archetypal form, with strong emotional content, similar to the Mandala, the circular Asian design for worship and symbolism, popularized in the West by Dr. C. G. Jung, Swiss founder of analytical psychology.

Agricultural experiments with pyramid shapes would, indeed, get it out of too cultist and faddish an atmosphere. Certainly, large-scale tests would have to be more tightly controlled than is the case with often fragmentary and amateurish experiments, long on enthusiasm but short on carefully planned, repeatable experimental design. Thousands of carefully controlled experiments on pyramids—and other shapes —would be required to provide a firm foundation for most of the claims now made. Firm control, detailed recording, and dispassionate evaluations are absolutely essential. When I first began the project of an anthology on pyramid power, a scientifically oriented, skeptical friend cautioned me not to engage in "fence-sitting comments" on the subject. That, he said, would be as if I were doing a book "about the earth being hollow at the poles, presenting both sides, and concluding that although the idea is far out, there may be something to it." Still, the pyramid power concept has captured the imagination of thousands. All they have to do is settle down to the kind of objective and exhaustive experimentation of which we still have too little. As for myself, I haven't used a razor blade in decades, being a firm devotee of the electric razor. Still, I've just heard of an experiment with a pyramid that sharpens electric razors; I am just waiting for a statistically valid experiment to confirm this claim.

M.E.

Twentieth-Century Pilgrimage

by Bob Brier

What happens when a New York professor of philosophy and teacher of Egyptology takes a small band of students to Egypt? Professor Brier, a member of the Department of Philosophy at C. W. Post College, made just such a pilgrimage to the pyramids. His witty and highly personal travelogue takes the reader, step by step, into the mystique and reality of pyramid territory. Brier conducts a course on Egyptian history and hieroglyphs at The New School, New York City.

"When the traveler has reached the top of the pyramids, his hands are torn and his knees are bleeding; he is surrounded by the desert and devoured by the light, and the harsh air burns his lungs; utterly exhausted, and dazzled by the brilliance, he sinks down half dead on the stone, amidst the carcasses of birds come there to die." In these thrilling words, French novelist Gustave Flaubert (1821–1880) described an ascent of the pyramids. However, Flaubert, an imaginative romanticist, had not yet been to Egypt when he concocted this description; only four years later did he make his famous pilgrimage to the pyramids.

I couldn't help thinking of Flaubert's colorful account when, in 1975, I led a small group of students up the west face of the Great Pyramid. When we reached the top, we were a bit tired, but no one had bleeding knees; the air was rather pleasant, and not a single bird was in sight, dead or alive. Amazingly, however, there was a small pile of camel dung; we wondered how it got there!

Flaubert had to wait four years until his legs caught up

with his imagination. Not a long time, really. I had to wait a good deal longer. Most people wait a lifetime and never get to see them. I had been a closet Egyptologist for years, only daring to express my interest in ancient Egypt with an occasional visit to New York's Metropolitan Museum where I would spend a few hours in the Egyptian section; or, perhaps, I'd stay up late to watch Boris Karloff revive Karis the mummy with tanna leaves.

My career as a professional Egyptologist started at a basketball tournament. While I was going up for a rebound, I was bumped from the side, and as I hit the floor, the ligaments and cartilage that held my kneecap in place were separated, never to meet again. An operation was needed. For six weeks, I was in a cast from ankle to hip. To help me pass the time, a friend gave me a copy of Sir Allan Gardiner's *Egyptian Grammar*. For six weeks I drew ducks, feet, owls, and other hieroglyphs. By the time the cast was removed I would be able to read the inscription in Tutankhamen's tomb, if only I could get there. Several years later I was teaching college courses in Egyptian hieroglyphs and ancient Egyptian philosophy, but still had not seen the pyramids.

For reasons I still can't explain, the pyramids are the most fascinating of all the ancient monuments. In the classes I teach I am asked more questions about the pyramids than all other aspects of Egypt combined. In the spring of 1974 I decided it was time I saw them.

There were problems of time and money. I was teaching Egyptology courses at C. W. Post College and the New School for Social Research. The only possible time to go would be intersession. The weather would be ideal in late December and early January, when the temperature in Cairo is in the seventies. So the time was fixed. The trip would be expensive, especially since there would be two of us. My wife, Barbara, though not a pyramid freak, recognized an adventure when she saw one and was to be a more than willing companion. The air fare was the big thing, but if one really wants to cut costs, there are ways. The Coptic Church (the Egyptian Christians) sponsors charter flights at almost half price for its members. Father Gabriel, head of the Coptic Church in the United States, was a friend, and Barbara and I quickly joined the Coptic Church's Social Club.

From friends who had been to Egypt I knew which were the hotels to stay in and wrote for reservations. A must in Cairo was the Mena House, at the foot of the pyramids. All hotels replied that there were no vacancies. We would have to go without reservations and take our chances. I later learned that there were vacancies; it is stock procedure for the hotels to write that they are full. Why, I don't know. Perhaps it is a test, so that only the truly eager and deserving get to see the pyramids!

I casually mentioned to one of my classes that I was going to Egypt in December. Soon word got out on campus, and I was being begged by students to take them along! If only I would take them, they would dig up the money. Pyramid fever was sweeping the dorms. After a quick conference with the Dean of C. W. Post, it was agreed that I would teach a special three-credit course in Egypt over intersession. I could take my students and get paid, too! My pilgrimage to the pyramids would not be a solitary one.

Selecting the students was a problem. Lots of people wanted to go, but I had to keep the size of the group manageable. I decided upon fifteen as this was the smallest number we could have and still get group rates. The selection process was crucial. The Middle East is a difficult area to travel in, and Egypt is no exception. I knew that mishaps would be the norm, and I couldn't afford to take inflexible people. I knew many of my former students would be good travelers. I later learned just how good, when we wound up sleeping four in a room on floors and cots! I quickly acquired a diverse group of adventurers.

Barbara and I had intended to show up in Egypt without reservations and take our chances, but with fifteen of us this was too risky. We found a travel agent who said he could get us reservations and we let him make our arrangements. Later he let us down, but that's another story. Everyone ran around getting visas and inoculations. We had a group meeting at our house so everyone could meet.

On December 29 we were at John F. Kennedy Airport for the departure of the charter flight. We were about the only non-Arabs on the flight, and this was our first taste of what Egypt was going to be like. The sheet of instructions we had all received clearly indicated that each passenger was allowed sixty-six pounds of baggage. The man ahead of me on the check-in line had two huge trunks and four truck tires as his baggage, and compared to some of the others he was traveling light. No one's baggage was ever weighed. After a two-hour wait, Father Gabriel blessed us and we boarded.

I was delighted when I found out that our seats were on the left side of the plane. If we followed the usual flight pattern, we would be able to see the pyramids from our window as we approached Cairo. They were eighteen hours away.

For plane reading I had brought E. I. S. Edwards's *The Pyramids of Egypt*, the standard work on the subject. My experience has been that although there are many pyramid enthusiasts around, they rarely take the time to read the solid, basic works on the subject. Most think that the pyramids are the culmination of the Ancient Egyptian civilization; actually they were built during the Old Kingdom, one of the earlier points in Egyptian history.

It is difficult to comprehend how long the Egyptian civilization lasted. The time of Christ seems distant to us, but there were pharaohs of Egypt to whom the pyramids were equally distant. The roughly three thousand years of ancient Egyptian history is divided into three major periods: Old Kingdom, Middle Kingdom, and New Kingdom. Before the Old Kingdom period began, the Nile Valley was settled by prehistoric man, sometime around 10,000 B.C. The dwellers on the plateaus that form the walls of the valley came down to live on the banks of the Nile. Although they were surrounded by desert, these people were not desert dwellers. They stayed along the Nile banks and rarely went into the desert. These first settlers of what we now call Egypt built small dwellings of mud brick, developed pottery, and flourished along the fertile banks of the river.

Eventually two separate kingdoms developed, one for Upper Egypt and one for Lower Egypt. This distinction between Upper and Lower Egypt is always confusing at first, *especially* if one looks at a map. Upper Egypt is beneath Lower Egypt! The reason is that the Nile flows the wrong way. Of all the major rivers of the world, it alone flows from south to north. The "upper" and "lower" refers to whether you have to go upstream or downstream to reach that part of Egypt.

The kingdoms, though culturally similar, were politically distinct. The king of Upper Egypt wore the white crown while the king of Lower Egypt wore the red crown of authority.

A politically divided Egypt existed for hundreds of years until one of the most important events in the history of ancient Egypt occurred: Narmer, the ruler of Upper Egypt, conquered Lower Egypt and united the two lands. For the first time in history, Lower and Upper Egypt were one; now, there was sufficient manpower to dominate the Near East for three thousand years, and soon there would be a strong enough central government to oversee the building of the pyramids.

Our knowledge of Narmer and his conquest is extremely sketchy and is based primarily on an inscribed palette. The Egyptians used stone palettes to grind the ingredients for their cosmetics. Sometimes, to commemorate an important event, an oversized palette was made and on it would be carved the story of the great event. Narmer's is the most famous of these palettes. One side shows the king wearing the crown of Upper Egypt, smiting a captured foe who is about half Narmer's size. Above the pharaoh's head are two hieroglyphs, a chisel and a fish. The word for chisel in Ancient Egyptian is *nar*, and *mer* means fish, thus the conclusion that the king's name was Narmer. On the reverse side of the palette we see Narmer wearing both the red and white crowns—he is now ruler of both lands. Narmer is the first of what Egyptologists call dynastic rulers; it is from Narmer that Egypt's dynasties are reckoned; he is the first king of the First Dynasty.

During the first two dynasties (this period is called Protodynastic), no pyramids were built. Instead, the pharaohs were buried in *mastabas,* a term derived from modern Arabic. Mastabas are the benches one sees outside modern Egyptian homes, where the owner might have evening coffee with his guests. The tombs of the pharaohs look quite a bit like these benches. The kings of the Protodynastic period were buried underground in a pit with a superstructure of mud brick. The underground burial chamber was divided into several compartments where the deceased and a few prized possessions were buried. Above ground, the mastaba had many more compartments, often as many as twenty-seven. These miniature stone houses were needed to contain all the supplies the pharaoh would need in his afterlife. It is out of these mastabas that the first pyramid developed: the step pyramid of King Zoser of the Third Dynasty.

The name of the architect of the first pyramid is known: Imhotep. Imhotep was a genius in several fields. He was Zoser's vizier, chief physician, and sage, and probably had several other titles. He was so renowned for his healing abilities that the Greeks deified him two thousand years later as their god of healing, Asclepius.

Zoser's pyramid is in the form of one mastaba placed upon another, upon another, upon another, and so on for six tiers. The stepped pyramid, aside from being the first pyramid, is the first monument built in stone, thus giving Imhotep another credit: he was the first to conceive of building in stone where previously mud brick alone had been used. The Egyptian priest Manetho, writing in the third century B.C., said of Imhotep that, "because of his medical skill he has the reputation of Asclepius among the Egyptians and was the inventor of the art of building with hewn stone."

The step pyramid is not an isolated monument in the middle of the desert. Although Zoser was buried beneath the pyramid, the pyramid was connected to a complex of stone buildings and courtyards intended for the king's use in the Netherworld. There were mortuary temples and enclosed courts, but perhaps the most important to Zoser was his *heb-sed* court. The *heb-sed* festival was probably a carry-over from remote times when a king was permitted to reign for only a limited period of time and then was ceremonially put to death. (During remote times, the king was expected to lead his armies in battle, and so it was crucial to the existence of the people that the ruler be young and physically fit.) The *heb-sed* festival enabled the king, by demonstrating his skill at wrestling, running, etc., to be magically rejuvenated and remain fit to rule. Zoser's *heb-sed* court must have been constructed by Imhotep, so that the pharaoh could perform the ceremony in the afterlife and remain vigorous for eternity.

It is likely that the pharaoh was pleased with his architect's creation. At Saqqara, near the step pyramid, a fragment of a statue of Zoser was found. On it is an inscription naming Imhotep as the king's vizier, architect, and physician. With such recognition, it is probable that Zoser permitted Imhotep the honor of placing his own mastaba near the pharaoh's pyramid.

For almost twenty years Walter B. Emery, an Egyptologist with the Egypt Exploration Society, searched for the tomb of the legendary Imhotep. The search started when

Emery noticed large quantities of broken potsherds on the ground not far from the pyramid. The pottery dated from the third century B.C., over two thousand years after the death of Imhotep but a period when he was enthusiastically worshiped. Emery reasoned that the pottery must have indicated a well-traveled route. The fragments couldn't have come from a dwelling, as the step pyramid is on the west bank of the Nile and the west bank was reserved for the dead. This probably stems from the early belief that the sun died each day in the west and was reborn each morning in the east. Emery concluded that the pottery indicated a pilgrimage route to the tomb of Imhotep. He started excavating.

During years of digging at Saqqara, Emery made several important discoveries, but did not find the tomb of Imhotep. But his last discovery may indicate that he was hot on the trail; he found a catacomb running for miles beneath the sand. Throughout the catacombs were mummified ibises perhaps over a million of them. The ibis was a bird sacred to Imhotep; Toth, the god of knowledge, is depicted as a man with the head of an ibis. Pilgrims probably placed the mummified birds as an offering at Imhotep's tomb. Emery was sure that somewhere at the end of the catacombs was the resting place of the architect of the first pyramid. He started clearing rubble that had accumulated in the passages and discovered that the tunnels were even more extensive than he had thought. He was forced to stop the digging because of the poor quality of the rock and the danger of a cave-in. Emery started digging nearby but died without finding Imhotep's tomb.

It was neither the step pyramid of Zoser nor Imhotep's tomb that was first on my list of things to see in Egypt. Above all, I wanted to see the Great Pyramid, and I was getting nearer.

After a stopover in Paris, the remainder of the flight seemed endless. The babies never went back to sleep and neither did anyone else. Finally, at 6:00 P.M. Cairo time, we were nearing the pyramids. I kept looking out my window hoping to catch a glimpse of them as we descended. Suddenly, there they were. They looked smaller than I had expected; one doesn't expect the Great Pyramid to look small even from a plane window. I could see the Great Pyramid and the two other large ones near it. They cast what seemed like extremely long shadows on the sand. Too quick ly they were out of sight, and we were coming down for a landing.

Cairo airport was teeming with people. This was a pilgrimage time, and thousands upon thousands of pilgrims were crowded behind two ropes between which we walked. A slightly heavy bald man in a tired gray suit came up and asked if we were the Lucky Tour group. Lucky Tours was the agent in Egypt who was handling our arrangements, and I was delighted to see this man. It was confirmation that such an organization really existed. All tour agencies in Egypt have distinctively non-Arabic names. The man, Mr. Latiff, asked me to collect everyone's passport. I gave him the pile and he ushered us through customs.

There was an interminable wait for the luggage, but finally all the bags were loaded on one handcart and a porter was wheeling it out an exit with Latiff screaming at him in Arabic. The stacking of the bags in the cart was fantastic. Over thirty bags were stacked in the most efficient manner possible, making a pile about seven feet high. One could tell it was a point of honor with the porter to use only one cart.

We were led to our buses, two old Mercedes with signs taped on the front, LUCKY TOURS. Our baggage was again efficiently stacked, this time on the luggage racks on the tops of the buses. It was now dark and we were all crashing; jet-lag had taken its toll. We stared out the bus windows, half in a daze. We could see barefoot boys driving donkey carts and small automobiles whizzing by them. Our driver forced pedestrians to scamper out of the way with each turn. I had chosen our Cairo hotel, the Mena House, with an eye toward the pyramids. The Mena House is located at the foot of the Great Pyramid, and with luck we would be able to see it from our hotel windows.

As we sped on our way to the hotel, someone said, "Look! The pyramids." It was quite dark and we were now on the outskirts of Cairo, so there were no street lights. Still, in the darkness one could make out the pyramids. It was almost as if one didn't see them, but rather felt their massiveness.

We arrived at the Mena House and checked in. There were the usual problems. A German group was supposed to have checked out, but their train reservations fell through, so they stayed another night. Some of our group wound up sleeping four in a room, but they didn't care. We were at the foot of the pyramids and could see them from the balconies of our rooms. Despite our exhaustion, being so close to the pyramids was too much; four of us decided to take the short walk to see them.

To get to the Gizeh pyramids from the Mena House one walks up a winding road lined with tourist shops. The owners are definitely high-pressure salesmen and practically drag you into their shops, offering free mint tea. This, however, was not the time to shop for souvenirs.

Quickly I walked up the hill to the pyramids and before I realized it, I was thirty feet from the Great Pyramid. The area was fairly deserted, but soon I was accosted by a local huckster. He came up to me and smiled a gold- and missing-toothed smile. He was a wiry little man who must have been in his sixties.

"Come. I show you pyramid. Very interesting."

"No thanks. I'd rather see it myself."

"Come. I show you pyramid. Very interesting."

"No thanks."

"Come. Very interesting."

I was tired and took the path of least resistance. He led me up the stairs that have been carved into the pyramid to allow the tourists to climb the twenty or so feet to the entrance. When we got there, it was barred by a locked iron gate. My guide lit a small stub of a candle and held it to the gate. I could see nothing. He told me that this was the Pyramid of King Cheops, and my tour was over. Very interesting.

Since I hadn't time to change any money yet, I gave him an American quarter and started to walk away. He complained that it wasn't enough and I refused to give him more. He persisted. I was tired and irritable and shouted at him that it was more than he deserved since I wanted to be alone anyway. Immediately a man with a rifle strapped to his back appeared. He too shouted at my unfortunate guide, for whom I was now feeling sorry. The man with the rifle was apparently a guard. As my guide was being run off, he turned, smiled, and said, "You got American cigarette?" and disappeared into the night. Finally I was alone but too tired to enjoy it. I walked slowly back to the Mena House for some needed sleep. I had finally seen the Great Pyramid.

The jump from the step pyramid to the true pyramid has not been an immediate one. Zoser was a Third Dynasty pharaoh, and it was during the Fourth Dynasty that the transition occurred. About thirty miles south of the step pyramid is the Pyramid of Meidum. It is badly damaged and today looks like a stepped pyramid with only two layers. During its construction it underwent several transformations. At first, there were seven steps, but later the base was enlarged and an additional step was added. But it did not remain this way; during the last stage of construction, the steps were filled in, making it a true pyramid. What remains today are two of the steps, with several steps still buried under sand.

The pharaoh for whom the pyramid was constructed is not known for sure. Like the earlier pyramids, this one too has funerary temples nearby, where priests performed rites to insure the king's well-being in the next world. In one of the temples are graffiti, written by an Egyptian of the Seventeenth Dynasty. One scrawling reads: "On the twelfth day of the fourth month of summer in the forty-first year of the reign of Tuthmosis III, the scribe Aa-Kheper-Resenb, son of Amenmesu, came to see the beautiful temple of King Sneferu. He found it as though heaven were within it and the sun rising in it." Thus, in all probability the Meidum Pyramid was Sneferu's.

Perhaps the most important feature of the Meidum Pyramid is that the north face contains an entrance-way that leads downward to the pharaoh's burial chamber. This passageway makes an angle of twenty-eight degrees with the ground, and when one was inside the pyramid looking out of the passage, it pointed like a telescope to the North Star. It no longer points to the North Star because of the changing position of the earth relative to the stars, but in the time of Sneferu it did. This feature, repeated in later pyramids, led some to speculate that the pyramids were used as observatories. Perhaps a more likely explanation is that the North Star, which, unlike other stars, does not seem to rotate during the night, was viewed with special reverence, and the passage was intended to allow the pharaoh to look out on it from his tomb.

Another interesting feature of the Meidum Pyramid is that, for the first time, the burial chamber is aboveground within the body of the pyramid. This pyramid may not have been Sneferu's only one.

A few miles south of Saqqara is Dashur, where another unique pyramid can be found, the Bent Pyramid. This pyramid is larger than Zoser's or the Meidum Pyramid. When construction began, it was intended that the sides slope inward at about fifty-four degrees. When the bottom third of the pyramid was completed, the angle was changed to a less steep forty-three and a half degrees, thus giving the pyramid its name, the Bent Pyramid.

The Bent Pyramid is unique because it has two separate entrances and two burial chambers. No sarcophagus or mummy was ever found in either chamber; the pyramid was almost certainly looted in ancient times. Like its predecessors, the pyramid has a complex of temples and courts connected to it, but they still lie under the sand. This pyramid has been given comparatively little attention by excavators.

Less than two miles from the Bent Pyramid is a pyramid known, because of the color of the exposed stone, as the Red Pyramid. This pyramid was built soon after the Bent Pyramid and the builder of this one seems to have learned from the problems with the Bent Pyramid. The slope of the sides of the Red Pyramid is forty-three and a half degrees, the same as the top of the Bent Pyramid. Near the Red Pyramid an inscription was found which mentions Sneferu and says he had two pyramids. Because of this, it has been assumed that the Meidum Pyramid and the Red Pyramid were his. Recently, excavations at the Bent Pyramid have established that it was built by Sneferu! So it appears we may have a pharaoh who had three pyramids.

It was not uncommon for a king to have two pyramids: one representing his rule over Lower Egypt and one his authority over Upper Egypt, but three is difficult to explain. The answer may be that for all practical purposes he really only had two. When the Meidum Pyramid collapsed, it was abandoned, unfinished, and so Sneferu had only two completed pyramids, the Bent and the Red.

It was Sneferu's son, Khufu, who built the Great Pyramid. There is some confusion about his name since the Greeks called him Cheops. Each pharaoh wrote his name in a cartouche, an oval enclosed by a symbolic rope to indicate the king's dominion. Khufu wrote his name in a cartouche that transliterates to Khufu, but the confusion with "Cheops" persists. If you go to the Metropolitan Museum of Art in New York, you will see a stone in the Egyptian wing which has the pharaoh's cartouche; the label gives the name as "Cheops."

Although many people think there are great mysterie

connected with the pyramids, Egyptologists have a pretty good idea of when, how, and by whom they were built.

The Great Pyramid is composed of about two and a half million blocks of granite averaging approximately two and a half tons each. It took about twenty-two years to build the pyramid, but no one is really sure how many men worked on it at one time. Herodotus, a Greek historian who visited Egypt in the fifth century B.C., states that 100,000 men worked on it three months at a time. Perhaps there were three-month shifts of duty with 100,000 men replacing another 100,000. However, this seems unlikely since there is no obvious need for rotation. Probably what he meant was that during the three months when the Nile overflowed its banks and no agricultural work was possible, men were free from their normal duties, and during these three months they worked on the pyramid, so that the work force swelled to 100,000. During the non-inundation months, the work force was probably considerably smaller.

Among the wide variety of skills needed in the construction of the Great Pyramid, probably the most important was masonry. There are several quarries in Egypt, and it was in these quarries that a considerable portion of the work was done. The masons, using copper chisels, cut the blocks from the quarry walls. Often a wooden wedge was forced into a crack in the wall and soaked with water. As the wedge absorbed the water, it expanded, and the wall cracked, freeing a block for the masons to finish. The stonework on the Great Pyramid is certainly the best of all the pyramids. This accounts for its excellent state of preservation. The blocks are almost perfectly squared, and to this day it is difficult to fit a knife blade between two adjacent stones of the pyramid. If the stones out of which a pyramid are built are almost perfectly squared, then the only force they will exert is a downward one. If, however, the stones are not carefully squared, they will exert lateral forces, to the left or right. If the outward force is great enough, a landslide will start, as in the case of the Meidum Pyramid.

The stones were almost certainly dressed at the quarry. This would lighten the load transported to the pyramid site. Although Egyptian civilization was quite advanced, the wheel had not yet been invented. Consequently, stones were hauled on sleds. Although there are no ancient papyri that show pyramid blocks being hauled, there are some that show colossal statues being transported in this manner. Oil was constantly poured in front of the sleds to reduce friction. If a site were far from the quarry, stones would be hauled to the Nile, placed on barges, and floated downstream. When the barges reached the part of the Nile nearest the pyramid site, they were unloaded and once again placed on sleds to be pulled across the sand.

The pyramid itself does not rest on sand, but on bedrock beneath the sand. For a structure so large (the base of the Great Pyramid covers over thirteen acres), the pyramid is amazingly level. No corner of the base is more than half an inch higher or lower than any other corner. This near-perfect leveling was achieved by digging a narrow trench around the circumference of what was to be the base of the pyramid. The trench was left open at the four corners and filled with water. Whichever corner the water ran out of was the lowest, and the other sides would be leveled till the water remained in the trench. This technique is quite similar to using a carpenter's level where water is enclosed in glass.

With the base level, blocks could be placed on bedrock and the construction started. It was during the construction of the lower portion of the pyramid that most of the manpower was needed. When the pyramid reached considerable height, large numbers of men couldn't have access to the top since the area worked on was relatively small. Often when people think about the labor involved in constructing the Great Pyramid, images are conjured up of slaves pulling furiously on ropes while being whipped by an Egyptian overseer. Actually, all available evidence indicates that the pyramid was built with free labor, men who voluntarily worked on the construction. There are blocks that were marked at the quarries that indicate the work crews' names. Such names as "Vigorous Crew," "Craftsmen Crew," and "Enduring Gang" indicate a pride taken in the work by the men who built the Great Pyramid.

Slaves never played a significant role in Egypt's economy. Although the Book of Exodus in the Old Testament clearly indicates that there were large numbers of Hebrews who were enslaved by a pharaoh, there is no archaeological evidence to support this. It was extremely difficult in ancient times to keep large numbers of slaves working under the watch of a few captors since there was no weapon, such as a gun, that could give a tremendous advantage to an outnumbered guard.

One of the interesting mechanical problems was raising the

blocks to the upper level. The Great Pyramid is as tall as a forty-five-story building with a slope of approximately fifty-two degrees. This is far too steep and long to pull a two-and-a-half-ton block up. There are two reasonable possibilities as to how the blocks were raised. A long approach ramp could have been built so that the angle of incline would have been gentle enough to pull the stones up and set them in place. The second method may have been to build a ramp around the pyramid in much the same way that a mountain road winds around the mountain. This too has the effect of making the angle of incline, up which the blocks have to be hauled, less steep. Herodotus said that the stones at the top were raised by machines. If what he said was true (the Great Pyramid was two thousand years old in Herodotus's time), then levers may have been used, but there is no evidence to support this.

When the core of the pyramid was completed, casing stones of polished white limestone were placed on the outside, and the exterior was glistening white in the sun. The interior of the pyramid was apparently intended to house the body of the pharaoh, but no body was ever found. Here there are some mysteries. There are actually two chambers in the Great Pyramid. The top chamber is known as the King's Chamber, but the only thing ever found in it was an empty stone sarcophagus with no markings. Thus we can't be sure that Khufu's body was ever in it. There are grooves on the top of the granite coffer which seem to indicate that there was a sliding lid, but no trace of the top was ever found.

Beneath the King's Chamber is the Queen's Chamber. The name, "Queen's Chamber," is probably derived from the gabled ceilings over the chamber. The Arabs bury their women in tombs with gabled ceilings and their men in tombs with horizontal ceilings. There is no real reason to believe that a queen was ever buried in the pyramid. Indeed, if both Khufu and his queen were buried in the same pyramid this would require sealing it twice, unless both queen and king died at the same time. It is interesting that the east wall in the Queen's Chamber has a recessed niche large enough to hold an upright sarcophagus. This room is also about the right proportion (eighteen feet by eighteen feet) to have been used as a storeroom for some of the pharaoh's possessions to be used in the next world, so there are many uses that can be speculated upon.

One can't help wonder why nothing of value has been found in the pyramids. Some feel that it is doubtful that the pharaohs were ever buried in them. It is true that Sneferu had at least two pyramids and couldn't have been buried in both. But a more likely explanation for the lack of treasures is grave robbers. Of all the burials of Egypt's pharaohs, only Tutankhamen's tomb escaped pillage, and there are even indications that it was robbed but resealed. The Great Pyramid was probably sacked in the First Intermediate Period. After the period known as the Old Kingdom, there was a total collapse of the strong central government and for a period of about 140 years there was general lawlessness. This is almost certainly the period during which the contents of the Great Pyramid were removed.

The contents of the Great Pyramid have, for over two thousand years, been the subject of considerable fantasy. In the ninth century A.D. the Arab adventurer Al Mamun, convinced that the Great Pyramid contained fantastic treasures, hired a band of men to break into it. The limestone blocks were too hard for the chisels he had, so fires were built against the stone and doused with cold vinegar till the heated stones cracked and in this way a tunnel over 100 feet long was made. Finally the men hit the descending passageway and eventually discovered the treasureless chambers. One of the 1001 tales of the *Arabian Nights* tells of Al Mamun's quest and gives the modern reader an idea of the fantastic legends that surround the Great Pyramid.

"The ancients say that, in the western Pyramid, are thirty chambers of vari-colored granite, full of precious stones and treasures galore and rare images and utensils and costly arms, which latter are anointed with magical unguents, so that they may not rust till the day of Resurrection."

One can't help but wonder about the frequently made claim that Al Mamun found treasure, but exactly equal to fair wages for breaking into the Great Pyramid. Some think that when he found nothing, he was afraid his men would riot without reward and secreted money in one of the chambers to pay them.

A few centuries after Al Mamun's forced entrance into the pyramid, the Great Pyramid was to suffer an even greater disfigurement. The Moslems near Cairo stripped the pyramid of its outer casing of polished white limestone in order to build their mosques. Today Cairo still has many beautiful white mosques, built from the outer face of the Great Pyramid. When the smooth surface was removed, this left the stepped interior, which is how the pyramid appears today.

My first daylight encounter with the Great Pyramid was much better than my nocturnal visit. When you see the pyramid up close, it is overwhelming and you don't know how to react—climb on it, stand back, or what. But you don't have long to decide anyway. As soon as you approach the pyramid, there is an onslaught of hustlers eager to have you ride their camel, take their picture, or sell you a fake antiquity. Of the hundreds of "antiquities" I have been offered for sale at the foot of the pyramid, I have never seen a genuine one. Usually small *ushabtis* are being sold by Arab children as genuine. The ancient Egyptians were buried with small statues of servants. They believed that in the next world they might be called upon to do work, and to avoid doing it they had 365 of these little statues—one for each day—to do the work for them. On the front of these *ushabtis* (Egyptian for "servant") was a magic spell which usually went something like this: "If I be called, or if I be assigned to do any work whatsoever of the labors which are to be done in the Other World . . . let the assignment fall upon you instead of me always, in the matter of sowing the fields, of filling the water courses with water, and of bringing the sands of the east to the west. 'Here I am!' shall you say."

Travelers are permitted to go inside the Great Pyramid. The entrance is through the opening that Al Mamun forced in the ninth century. There are electric lights inside now, but it is not difficult to imagine the feeling the early adventurers who entered the pyramid must have had. If one is claustrophobic, it is best not to go in. To get to the King's Chamber you have to go up the ascending passageway, which is only four feet high and four feet wide and slopes upward at an angle of twenty-six degrees. For more than 150 feet you are crouched over, slowly moving upward, fearful of bumping your head or having to stand upright to relieve back pain and not being able to. Finally the narrow passage ends, and what is called the Grand Gallery begins. The Grand Gallery continues the twenty-six-degree slope and four-foot width but is twenty-eight feet high and it too continues for about 150 feet. No one is sure of the original purpose of this passageway. At the end there is a sudden three-foot step up, and the floor levels but the ceiling drops to less than four feet! The low ceiling continues for less than ten feet and then one is in a small antechamber, leading to the King's Chamber.

There is a facet of the Great Pyramid that many tourists overlook—the boat pits. The pharaohs of ancient Egypt were buried with boats which were to take them to the next world. It is not surprising that a boat would be used for the journey since the boat was the primary means of transportation in Egypt. The Egyptians were not desert nomads riding camels through the sands. They stayed close to the Nile.

There are five boat pits around the Great Pyramid. Three were known to exist for quite some time and had been empty probably since antiquity. All that was ever found in them were fragments of gilded wood and pieces of rope. In the early 1950's excavation revealed two more pits on the south side of the pyramid. These were still sealed with limestone blocks weighing over fifteen tons each. A hole was drilled in one of the blocks, and through the darkness pieces of a boat could be seen. When the sealing blocks were removed, a boat in kit form was revealed. It was in almost perfect condition after having been in the airtight chamber for 4,500 years. The boat has been reconstructed and measures over 120 feet in length. It was almost certainly never used and was intended for only one trip—to take Khufu to the Netherworld. The second pit remains sealed and may house the boat that the pharaoh used in this world.

After we visited the Great Pyramid, several of us wanted to climb to the top. We were told repeatedly by local authorities and natives that it was dangerous and illegal. "Last year an American fell off and was killed." It really didn't seem dangerous since the stones were sound and no real climbing had to be done. Because of the stepped construction it would be much like climbing a giant's staircase; just pull yourself up, step by step. Our group had even been approached by a handsome blue-eyed Arab guide who offered to take us to the top. His name was Shedde, and I promised him that if we did climb the pyramid, we would ask for him. Even though it looked easy, I thought it would be well worth the small fee we would have to pay him to have him show us the easiest route.

When we made the decision to climb the pyramid, we

asked around for Shedde, and soon he appeared. When I asked him his price, he went into a long explanation about how *some* people pay him five Egyptian pounds (about $10) each, but that was too much. I agreed. Bargaining is an Arab custom and one is always told a ridiculous price at first. We finally settled on five pounds for the group with a good tip when everyone returned in one piece.

When it came time to start the ascent, a few of the group were riding camels and horses and couldn't be found. Most of the nonclimbers found a comfortable spot at the foot of the pyramid and settled in. We figured it would take about two hours round-trip. Shedde told us that the record for climbing to the top was seven minutes. He was one of the few guides who didn't claim to hold this record.

We started climbing slowly, taking big steps up the blocks. We were at about the tenth layer of stones when one climber decided she had had enough and headed down. Another two layers and we lost another who decided to sit there and wait for us when we came down. There were now just four of us with Shedde. Shedde and I went first, helping the others up, but no one really had any difficulty. Even looking down was not frightening; it was not a sheer drop, like looking over a cliff. There was always a lower step about three feet below which gave the feeling of security. It seemed as if the most you could fall was three feet.

When we were about two thirds of the way up, a group of schoolboys who seemed about ten years old came rushing by us! They were laughing and joking as if they did this every day after school. Great adventurers we were. We continued to the top and rested there and enjoyed the view. The very uppermost of the pyramid's stones are gone now, so there is an area of about twenty feet by twenty feet which is level. We could see Kephren's Pyramid almost at eye level, and in the far distance was the Bent Pyramid at Dashur. The Great Sphinx actually looked like a toy. I was astounded by the row upon row of neat orderly mastabas of nobles who were buried near the pyramids. From the ground one doesn't get a sense of the order and number of them. Getting down went more quickly than the ascent, and we all congratulated each other when we reached the bottom. The group that had remained at the bottom seemed quite relieved that we had made it safely. Actually, at no time was there any danger.

It is surprising that the Great Pyramid receives so much

more attention than the pyramid next to it. Kephren, son of
Khufu, built a pyramid only a few feet shorter than his
father's and it is equally impressive. When viewed from
one angle, it even looks taller because it is built on a high
portion of the Gizeh plateau. It is curious that Kephren
did not try to outdo his predecessor and build a slightly
larger pyramid. It was traditional to build bigger and more
numerous monuments than ever before. One theory is that
Kephren built a smaller pyramid out of respect for Khufu.
If this is true, it is unique.

Kephren's Pyramid can easily be distinguished from the
Great Pyramid since there is still a bit of the smooth limestone casing left at the top. The stones out of which the
pyramid was built are not of the same high quality as
Cheops's and when the limestone exterior was being stripped
away to build the mosques of Cairo, some of the lower
stones crumbled and it was impossible to climb to the top to
get the casing.

In front of Kephren's Pyramid is the Great Sphinx. There
are many sphinxes in Egypt with various forms. The Great
Sphinx was built by Kephren (2565–2542 B.C.) at the same
time his pyramid was under construction. When the cause-
way leading to the pyramid was being dug, a great sandstone
rock was uncovered. Rather than waste such a natural marvel, the workers carved the Great Sphinx. The body is that
of a lion and the head is of a man, almost certainly Kephren.

At the feet of the Great Sphinx is a stone tablet that tells
of a dream had by the young prince, Tuthmosis IV. The
young prince lived over a thousand years after the Sphinx was
carved, and by then it was almost completely covered with
sand. Tuthmosis was hunting and at noon he became tired
as he neared the Sphinx. He napped in its shade and
dreamed. In the dream the Sphinx spoke to him and told
him that if he removed the sand that encumbered it, he
would become pharaoh. Tuthmosis removed the sand and
later became pharaoh. To commemorate this prophetic
dream he erected the dream stela, as it is known, at the foot
of the Sphinx.

The third of the large Gizeh pyramids is that of Mycerinus
and is much smaller than the other two large pyramids. It
can serve, however, as an example of just how large the
pyramids are. The Arab historian Abd al Latif tells how in
the thirteenth century a caliph decided the pyramids should
be torn down. He amassed a huge working force from all

over the country and set them to work tearing down Mycerinus's Pyramid. After eight months of constant work, they gave up. Abd al Latif says, "Considering the vast masses that have been taken away, it might be supposed that the building would have been completely destroyed, but so immense is the pile that the stones are scarcely missed. Only on one of its sides can be noticed any trace of the impression which it was attempted to be made."

Near this pyramid are three relatively small subsidiary pyramids, none of which seems to have been completed. It is not known for whom they were built, but a good guess is the pharaoh's wives and/or daughters.

No one is sure why pyramid building stopped toward the end of the Old Kingdom, but Mycerinus's successor built a mastaba to house his body for eternity. Some feel that pyramid building stopped because of the decline of a strong central government and because large numbers of workers could not be paid to work on the monuments. Others believe that the halt in the building of the pyramids caused the decline since now there were large numbers of unemployed workers who became unruly. I favor the first theory; it seems more likely to me. Either way, after the Old Kingdom fell, Egypt was to rise again, but the age of pyramids was over.

The Pharaoh's Curse

by Gordon Thistlewaite

The pyramids of Egypt have been the focus of three elements of mystery: their supposed prophetic architectural aspects; their energy "powers," discussed throughout this volume; and the alleged curse specifically attributed to the tomb of one of the pharaohs, Tutankhamen. Mr. Thistlewaite examines the series of dramatic deaths that have been attributed to the Curse of Tutankhamen since his tomb was excavated by European archaeologists. Together with two other mysterious elements popularly connected with Egypt's pyramids, these events illustrate the unusual fascination the pyramids hold for scientists as well as the general public throughout the world.

In Cairo, Egypt, on Monday, December 19, 1966, a car struck down Mohammed Ibrahim, fracturing his skull and inflicting other injuries that caused his death two days later. Mr. Ibrahim, the Egyptian government's Director of Antiquities, was struck as he left a conference with French diplomats at the Ministry of Culture.

For four months Ibrahim had fought against Egypt's decision to send relics from the famous "cursed tomb" of Pharaoh Tutankhamen to an exhibition in Paris. When he finally concurred, his daughter was seriously injured in an auto smash-up. He began to have dreams that he was to die. Unnerved, he made an appointment with the Minister of Culture to seek reconsideration of the government's agreement. French representatives attended the meeting.

At the conference, Ibrahim was finally prevailed upon to withdraw his objection. It was pointed out that the government had, some months before, officially pronounced the curse to be only a superstition and out of keeping with socialist philosophy. However, as Mohammed Ibrahim left the meeting, superstition turned into reality as death bore down upon him with the swift wings of steel and iron.

The eighteen-year-old Pharaoh Tutankhamen had been buried with a splendor unmatched in Egypt both before and after his time. His tomb, uncovered thirty-three centuries later, was said to have had a curse attached to it. That rumor, which circulated even before the tomb was entered, gained credence with the extraordinary death of George E. S. M. Herbert, fifth Earl of Carnarvon who had financed and collaborated with archaeologist Howard Carter in searching for the tomb. Deaths occurred with disturbing frequency among those who had had anything to do with the opening of the burial place in the bleak and arid Biban-el-Maluk, the Valley of the Kings. A full listing would be impossible here, but the following may give an idea of why a sense of awe and uneasiness spread rapidly around the world.

Sir Archibald Douglas-Reid, the radiologist appointed to X-ray the mummy, died on his way to the tomb. Frank Raleigh, a photographer, went blind and died. Egyptologist H. E. Evelyn-White wrote a letter saying he knew there was a curse on him and committed suicide. Howard Carter's secretary died. He had taken from the tomb an alabaster vase which bore the inscription, "Death shall come on swift wings to him that toucheth the tomb of Pharaoh."

His father, Lord Westbury, inherited the vase. According to a dispatch from Universal News Service in February, 1930: "Lord Westbury was frequently heard to mutter, 'the curse of the pharaoh,' as though this preyed on his mind. In his last letter he wrote, 'I cannot stand this horror any more and am going to make an exit.'" Westbury threw himself from the window of his suite in London, plunging through a glass canopy on his way to instant death on the sidewalk. His funeral hearse struck and killed eight-year-old Joseph Greer on its way to the graveyard.

Many more deaths occurred among those who had visited the tomb. And yet, many who might have been expected to die, lived on to their normal life expectancy or beyond and then died of natural causes. Among these was Howard Carter, who actually opened the tomb and died at the age of sixty-seven in 1939. Professor James Breasted of the University of Chicago, said, "I defy the curse and if anyone was exposed to it, I was. I slept in that tomb for two weeks. I even had my meals there." Breasted lived to the age of seventy and died in 1935. Sir Flinders Petrie, the father of Egyptology, died at eighty-nine; Professor P. E. Newberry died at eighty; Sir Edward A. Wallis Budge died at seventy-seven. All had been prominent in examining the tomb and all died from natural causes.

At first glance, it would appear that one can find plenty of support for the belief in a curse on Tutankhamen's tomb and that, conversely, one can find just as much support for the idea's being only a superstition. But, as we are going to see, this does not allow for the modern occultist's understanding of how a curse works.

The only written curse on Tutankhamen's tomb was that inscribed on the alabaster vase that Lord Westbury inherited from his dead son. There is an apocryphal story that when Carnarvon found the vase, he put his hand inside it, drawing it out to discover blood on one of his fingers. This in itself could have launched the rumor of a curse, but the fact is that the existence of a curse was known well before that incident.

From the occult standpoint, a curse need not be written out; but, if it is reduced to writing and thus made known to the accursed, it becomes that much more effective. In fact, once known to the accursed individual, the curse may work through normal psychological means without reference to any occult force. Very frequently, though by no means always, Egyptian tombs were cursed. This we know not only from the literature of the times, but also from inscribed curses found on some of the tombs.

From literature, for example, we know some methods of imposing a curse. Powerful slaves, dedicated to the pharaoh, were slowly tortured until they were all but out of their minds. At the same time injunctions were read to them that they must continue to guard the pharaoh in the next life as they had in this. When they had been brainwashed with that idea, they were instantly killed. The feeling was that their anguished, single-minded spirits would make the most hostile tomb guardians. Of course, we can have no idea of how would like to believe.

Some curses did carry elaborate inscriptions. One on the mummy of Pharaoh Seti I began: "The cobras on my crown will spew flames of fire on him who disturbs my rest . . ." many tombs were cursed in this way. Perhaps more than we

There was another: "As for anyone who enters this tomb, my spirit will pounce upon him as on a bird and he shall be judged by the great god . . ." And yet another: "The Sun god shall punish him who injures my tomb or drags out my mummy . . ." Such inscriptions pale beside the malefic sophistication of the torture method, however, and this has always suggested to me that they were intended only to scare away the professional tomb robbers. In this they were not too successful for, according to the Abbot Papyrus, in the reign of Ramses IX, about 200 years after Tutankhamen, it was necessary to wage an all-out police campaign against the thieves.

But there is very good reason to believe that Tutankhamen's tomb was cursed and cursed with the most furious malediction possible. We'll find there was good reason for this, along with the mystery of why a do-nothing king whose only distinction, according to Howard Carter, was to die and get buried, should have received the most elaborate funeral in Egyptian history.

For sixteen years archaeologist Howard Carter and Lord Carnarvon, his backer, had looked for the tomb of Tutankhamen in the Valley of the Kings. They knew it was buried there because of the evidence of remnants of the funeral observance which bore the king's name. By November, 1922, the Carnarvon permit to explore was about to expire. He went to London. Carter, with only four days left, made one more try and found the buried stairway leading to the tomb.

He cabled Carnarvon in London and the peer, with his daughter Evelyn, went at once to Egypt. They watched as Carter made a hole and peered into the tomb. They had had only a glimpse into an antechamber, but it was filled with furniture of solid gold. And that was only the beginning. Clearing a tomb takes a lot of time. Every tiny detail must be photographed, measured, and catalogued before being moved. While the preliminary work was going on, Carnarvon and his daughter went back to England.

The London *Times* carried the story of the discovery, and it came to the attention of Count Louis Hamon, the famous psychic and palm-reader who went by the name of Cheiro. The very evening he read the story, he was visited by his guide, an Egyptian girl. The girl indicated a writing pad. Cheiro went into trance and produced through automatic writing a message which read: Lord Carnarvon must not enter tomb. If he does, he will suffer sickness and death will claim him in Egypt.

Cheiro wrote to Carnarvon at once, but the latter had his own seer, a man named Velma. Velma gave him a reading and summed up his findings, "I see danger for you, probably arising out of your interest in the occult." Carnarvon went away in a somber mood. He was a worried man. Before he left again for Egypt he saw Velma. This time Velma used a crystal ball.

Velma reported seeing an Egyptian scene. He saw a temple, mourners, and an aging priest placing a mask of gold on the head of a mummy. He saw the tomb with Carnarvon near it. Lightning flashes erupted from the tomb and enveloped Carnarvon until he was standing alone in their midst. Velma said, "I see disaster for you. Abandon the work." Carnarvon admitted that he had felt a strange influence at work, urging him to give up the project, but he refused to do so. With his daughter, he sailed back to Egypt.

There, before hundreds of spectators and newsmen, Carnarvon and his party prepared to open the tomb's second chamber. As the time arrived, he rose and said jestingly, "All right, everyone. I think we're ready for our little concert in the tomb." And one of the newspapermen said, "If he goes down in that spirit, I give him six weeks to live . . ."

One day as Carnarvon emerged from the tomb a mosquito bit him on the face. That was unusual because the valley is mosquito-free due to lack of water. The next morning, when Carnarvon was shaving with his straight razor, he nicked the mosquito bite. He dabbed at the spot with cotton and iodine; however, that evening he ran a temperature of 101 and felt a chill. He took to his bed. Some kind of poisoning was apparently at work. He was prostrate for ten days, then developed pneumonia and died. At the moment Carnarvon died, every light in the city went out and stayed out for five minutes. The Cairo Electricity Board found fuses and circuit breakers intact and was never able to assign a reason to the eerie event.

Though the tomb was discovered in 1922, the careful progress of the archaeologists did not result in the opening of the king's coffin until late in 1925. And just as Velma had seen in his crystal ball three years earlier, the face of the mummy was covered by a lifelike mask of gold.

Now we come to the question of why an obscure pharaoh was given the most elaborate funeral in the history of Egypt? And why was so potent a curse apparently laid upon his tomb? The era from which Tutankhamen rose was a historical cesspool, a nightmare of vice and intrigue. It had its beginning nearly fifty years before when Pharaoh Amenophis III married Tiy, a princess of the Mitanni kingdom. The pharaoh's grandfather, Thutmose III, had grouped all priesthoods under the High Priest of Amon and made him great seer of the realm. As such he prophesied on state events. When a boy was born to young Tiy, the prophecy about him was such that his father had him raised in exile, probably at the court of Mitanni. After the child's birth his name never appeared in records until the death of his father, when he then returned to Egypt and assumed the throne. He brought with him the idea of a new religion which, of course, brought him into conflict with the High Priest of Amon. This, along with hating the priest for the prophecy that exiled him, resulted in the new pharaoh moving his court from Thebes to the north. He called his new capital Akhet-Aton. He dropped the word "Amon" from his name and called himself Akhnaton.

For a long time, history regarded Akhnaton as a heroic humanist, a great religious reformer. He banned all the gods of Egypt and made the state religion the worship of one god —Aton. He patronized poets and painters and, indeed, some of the artwork of his time, showing chiaroscuro and perspective, was not to be matched again until the Renaissance . . . In the meantime, he neglected his political responsibilities. His regents in Egypt's various dominions called on him vainly for help, but he was too wrapped up in art, poetry, religion, and his family life. Somewhat of a narcissist, he often had himself and his entire family portrayed in the nude. His wife was the beautiful Nefertiti, whose bust is one of the best-known pieces of sculpture in the world.

For twelve years Akhnaton let the empire crumble while he played with his family. Nefertiti bore him six daughters.

Archaeologists puzzled long over the presence of a seventh daughter who always seemed to be linked to Tiy, Akhnaton's mother, rather than to Nefertiti. They grew uneasy when they found that Tiy wore the double plumes of empire, and even more so when Tiy, not Nefertiti, bore the title of Great Wife. Shock followed when it was discovered that the seventh princess, Beketaten, was Tiy's child by her son Akhnaton. In short, the king's mother was now his wife and the mother of his daughter-sister. Nefertiti had been replaced.

Now two young princes appear upon the scene, Smenkare and Tutankhamen. We do not know for certain who their mothers were, but we can speculate. Scientists agree that they were both fathered by Akhnaton. It is my opinion, based on comparing the features of the princes with those of Tiy and Nefertiti, that Smenkare was Nefertiti's son and Tutankhamen was Tiy's.

Smenkare married Meritaten, one of Nefertiti's daughters; Tutankhamen married Ankhesenpaaton, another daughter, but not before she bore a child to her father. Akhnaton then appointed his son Smenkare co-ruler and, at the same time, appears to have been involved in an unnatural affair with him. At this point, something in the nature of a revolution occurred, though records on it are missing. We know only that Egypt was in dire trouble. There was a vast body of unemployed. The borders of the empire were crumbling and no more riches were flowing into the country. And the king himself was given to vices that were anathema to the Egyptians.

In the kingdom of Mitanni, from which Tiy came and where Akhnaton was raised, it was regarded almost as a religious sacrament for a son to have a child by his mother. The custom was known as *xvetokdas* and was the second of the seven good works of religion. But to the Egyptians, although they recognized second-degree marriages (brother/ sister), marriage in the first degree was an unspeakable sin. Akhnaton was deposed. Tiy killed herself—and Nefertiti vanished. None of their mummies has ever been found.

With Tiy's death and Akhnaton (probably) exiled, Smenkare now took over the throne, and Ay, Tiy's brother, became Chamberlain and Great Priest. Ay advised the king to make an expedition to strengthen his dominions and try to win back the border lands. While Smenkare was away (and it seems he never returned), Ay put his nephew, the twelve-year-old Tutankhamen on the throne, meanwhile plotting and planning the devious way in which he himself could gain total control. And so it happened that after six years the young boy mysteriously died at the age of eighteen, leaving his doe-eyed queen, Ankhesenpaaton, his sole survivor. Ay, by default, became the next pharaoh.

Carefully repeated, over and over again in Tutankhamen's tomb inscriptions tell how it was Ay who was responsible for the lavish entombment. He seems to have made sure he got the credit. Yet, as Howard Carter pointed out, at no other time in Egyptian history did a pharaoh ever take credit for burying a predecessor. Why then was this so?

Ay was afraid. The ancient Egyptians subscribed to severe

ethical beliefs. Before the spirit could pass through the Hall of Truth after death, it had to justify itself. Other souls could rise up against it, as Tutankhamen's could against Ay. But Ay had a way of buying himself off. The goal of the Egyptian was undisturbed rest among all the effects he might possibly need in the hereafter.

So Ay made sure that Tutankhamen would rest forever in the most lavishly equipped tomb in Egypt. He made sure nothing was wanting that might make the pharaoh's sleep restless, even to including a carefully labeled lock of hair from the head of his mother, Tiy. The spirit of the young pharaoh would have no reason to wander abroad in the night, nor would it rise up against Ay at the Judgment, forever barring him from Amenti.

But, as Velma is reported to have told Lord Carnarvon, "Wherever a place has been the focus of tremendous emotion, there is not the slightest doubt that something—I don't know what—persists." Thus, despite whatever powerful curse Ay laid on Tutankhamen's tomb, there was something else to be considered. The affair of Tutankhamen represented the point at which all of the wretched emotions of Akhnaton's court converged, all the incest, vice, depravity, and insanity, despair, and deceit; all the thwarted ambition, the treachery, the homicides, the suicides, the gnawing guilts were symbolized in that lavish entombment, fermenting like some evil wine, sealed in a bottle of gold.

Carnarvon and Carter uncorked that bottle.

We are still left with the problem of why Carnarvon died and not Carter; why Egyptologist Evelyn-White killed himself and Sir Flinders Petrie lived to be eighty-nine; why Carter himself was not affected, but Lord Westbury was driven to death by the mere presence of the vase. We know more today of the mechanics of a curse than we did fifty years ago. Papers on curse pathology appear in orthodox medical journals.

The late Adrian Dobbs, the mathematical genius of Cambridge University, saw a transfer of psychic energy in subatomic particles he named psitrons. Such a particle carries a "bit" of information to a critically poised neuron in a receptive subject, causing that neuron to fire. A chain reaction is set up; other neurons become involved and the subject perceives. The only condition for the interaction is that the first neuron be critically poised when the psitron hits.

We might guess then, if we allow Dobbs's theories, that

the maliciously charged psitrons saturating the tomb of Tutankhamen fired poised neurons in receptive nervous systems and passed harmlessly through others. That some profound psychic influence was at work is most directly evidenced by one fact. It was nearly three years after Carnarvon's death that Tutankhamen's mummy was unwrapped and examined by pathologists. They found on the cheek of the mummy a wound exactly like the mosquito bite that had caused Carnarvon's death!

Twenty Years in the
Shadow of the Pyramids

by James E. Kinnear

Captain Kinnear, born in New Zealand, went to Cairo, Egypt, in 1928 to share in the management of an educational publishing house that issued books and treatises in several languages, but for the most part in Arabic. He had specialized in languages and linguistics for his degrees at the University of Otago, New Zealand. World War II interrupted his career but did not take him out of the Middle East, where he first served with the British Arab Battalions and later at the British embassy in Cairo.

I made my first step in the direction of the pyramids in my late twenties, when I boarded a New Zealand Shipping Line vessel at Auckland in August, 1928. It took me some twelve hundred miles across the usually stormy Tasman Sea to Sydney, Australia. There I transferred to the P.&O. liner that plied between Sydney and Southampton, England, dropping me off at the northern end of the Suez Canal. From Port Said a fairly reliable train service took me up to Cairo, my destination. There were no airlines in operation in those days, and so the journey took twenty-eight days.

Arriving in Cairo about nine in the evening I was met by friends and driven to what would be my permanent address for several years in the heart of the great, sprawling metropolis—half modern and sophisticated and half ancient and rather poverty-stricken. It was on Sharia al-Manakh, a name which meant "A kneeling-place for camels"—no longer such but no stranger to those haughty pack animals weaving through the motor traffic in the modern sectors of the city.

Next morning I was awakened by the raucous cries of

45

newspaper boys supplying Cairenes with *Al-Ahram*, which is Arabic for "The Pyramids." Even then it was a formidable journal. When, in later years during my work at the British embassy, I came to know its editors, my respect for this quasi-official organ greatly increased. But on that first day I was a long, painful way from being able to read what it had to say. I soon learned, however, that *haram* (the singular of Ahram) meant "an object of [considerable] antiquity." It was significant that the Egyptians themselves did not give the pyramids a name that was any more specific, apparently sharing the uncertainty that bedevils scholars to this day as to their precise origin and purpose.

My excursion through the busy streets that first morning provided my first brush with the romance of early Egyptian history. We were in an open carriage and we paused a few moments at a spot on the shore of the Nile, now well within the city limits, where the infant Moses was discovered in the bulrushes by Pharaoh's daughter. At least that is the site around which the tradition has been woven.

A few blocks farther on, we were introduced to the director of the American University at Cairo. It was in this very beautiful structure, built in the authentic Arabian motif, that I was to spend a year and a half absorbing the stilted intricacies of classical Arabic, the easy-flowing colloquial of ordinary conversation, and the solemnly intoned cadences of *The Quran*, believed by Muslims to be the heaven-descended fount not only of the true faith but also of the "purest Arabic." It was the toughest linguistic assignment I had ever encountered. My chief supervisor at the School of Oriental Studies—a department of the American University—was Dr. Arthur Jeffery, who later came to New York to head the department of Oriental Studies at Columbia University.

One of the elements in the scene which early engaged my attention was the coexistence of two distinct ethnic groups in Egypt: Arabs and Copts. This situation dates from the Islamic invasion of Egypt over a ten-year period from 632–642 A.D. The Copts are distinguished by a lighter skin and slightly almond-shaped eyes. Their origin goes right back to the Pharaonic ages. Their ancestors helped build the pyramids. You see, the name Egypt derives from *Qypt* or *Gypt*, which is the ancient and present pronunciation of Copt. They are Christians, a minority living in the midst of a predominantly Muslim population.

By a strange turn of fate, the pyramids, which watched

the bloodless expulsion of the Hebrew people from the Valley
of the Nile under Thutmose III, witnessed also, in recent
years, the warring confrontations between Egypt and the
progeny of those Twelve Tribes of nomads who escaped the
pharaoh's chariots and horsemen.

Speaking of the historicity of the Old Testament, archaeologists have over the last hundred years been able to au-
thenticate a great many of the accounts given in that ancient
book as to battles fought, the location and fate of many of
the cities mentioned, movements of peoples, tribes, and so
forth. It is somewhat strange that the pharaoh of the Exodus
is not named in the Old Testament and the pyramids seem
only to lie behind one obscure phrase, "the Tower of Syrene,"
found in Ezekiel 29:10.

It may seem remarkable also that in the many thousands of
hieroglyphs uncovered, which encompassed the period of the
Hebrew exodus under the leadership of Moses, not one makes
mention of that historic event. But that is not so strange. It
was common practice among ancient historians to gloss over
or omit mention altogether of an event that reflected no glory
on the monarch of the day.

Our first visit to the pyramids was a memorable day. What
was then a twenty-minute taxi ride from the heart of the
city or a forty-minute streetcar excursion took us right into
the shadow of those imposing monuments. Today, buses cover
this route.

The official guides, or dragomans, do a flourishing business
escorting groups of tourists over the area expounding the
while, in several languages, the wonders of ancient Egypt as
exemplified in the pyramids and the Sphinx, which is close by.
Many ride camels for the tour, which lasts an hour or so, to
discover that the end of that journey brings them great relief
from a "nagging neck-ache" developed by the peculiar gait
of their mounts.

Many of the more hardy visitors elect to climb the great
Pyramid of Cheops, the highest and the only one on which
climbing is permitted. It is possible to use the huge stepping-
stones right to the top, whereas the next largest pyramid,
that of Kephren, right alongside, still is topped by many
courses of the original smooth casing. In World War II the
Army Command forbade all climbing of that pyramid to the
men in uniform. Some of them flouted the order and at least
two lost their lives.

No one may climb the Pyramid of Cheops without a

guide, and I advise no one who suffers from shortness of breath or chest pains of any kind to try it. Most of the steps are table-high, and the guide, in hopes of packing in an extra trip or two, is apt to hurry you unmercifully. At last one is on the summit, some four hundred and eighty feet above the base platform. Several of the coping blocks have been removed at one time so that one can walk about on a flat area some thirty feet square. In 1921, the Prince of Wales (later to be Edward the VIII) took along a golf club or two and a dozen balls so that he would be able to say when he got home that he had whacked them off the world's highest tee.

The view from the top is breathtaking, especially in view of the fact that there are few elevated spots in all Egypt and the wide outlook seems particularly novel. Away beyond the tall buildings of Cairo one sees the Mokattam Hills, whence were drawn the huge two-ton blocks that were used for the body of the pyramids.

That was brought home to me in 1944 when I was on the staff of the British embassy to Egypt. Tires were a very precious commodity in those war days and many a Cairo taxi-driver had to go out of business through inability to keep himself in tires. We at the embassy, being virtually part of the war effort, were given special privileges including new tires when needed. I drove over to the army supply depots in the Mokattam Hills and found that the ancient pharaonic stonemasons had been kind to us. Their huge removals of limestone from that area had created a network of enormous caves and passageways. And it was in those cool storehouses that the British army had built up a truly formidable reserve of tires of all sizes. In no time at all a sergeant tossed a fresh set of four into my car and I drove away as happy as a king.

Say, where did I leave you—on top of the pyramid? Well, if the climb to the apex was hard enough, the descent was very much worse. It was practically a matter of jumping from one course of stone to the one below almost the whole distance. After a score or two of those leaps you feel as if your knees will surely give out on the next jump. If your guides take your hand and do a little dragging to hurry you down, be firm. Tell them to jump in the river—which is conveniently close by! You will not offend them. Those good-natured fellows will get a good laugh out of that.

If you have a notion to go inside the pyramid, save it for

another day. You will toil up about one eighth of the south side and enter the Descending Passage. In my day, lighting was provided by flaming torches, since replaced by pressure lamps —and no doubt succeeded by electric lighting. Bats were a problem and ladies suffered nasty shocks when one of those creatures, with all their agility, got tangled in their hair! In the early days of exploration the bats were a double nuisance. They took refuge there in hordes and had created such a choking, ammoniacal stench with their droppings that explorers had to rush back into the open air to avoid suffocation. All that is fortunately a thing of the past. After the steep descent of the first passage, you come to a low point and begin climbing to a point where you may decide whether to do the whole tour, which is to visit both the Queen's Chamber, by a level passage, and the King's Chamber, by a steeply ascending one. Most tourists settle for the latter. After all, the pharaoh's burial chamber (which is what the guide will assure you it is) is the most romantic spot in that mysterious structure.

It is reported that Napoleon Bonaparte, in his Egyptian campaign against the Mamelukes, fought the decisive battle at the site of the pyramids. The ten thousand Mameluke horsemen were no match for the French sharpshooters and cannoneers. Two thousand Mamelukes were slaughtered on that fateful day; only twenty-four French were killed! Following the bloody encounter, Napoleon looked around and, with his logistical mind, figured that the Great Pyramid and its neighbors would provide enough stone to build a wall three meters high and a meter thick all around France.

But his interest went deeper. He was intrigued by stories that the King's Chamber had certain arcane qualities. When he and his entourage reached the pyramid he asked to be escorted to the chamber and left alone there for a time, as Alexander the Great was reported to have done before him. Napoleon must have had some strange experience there, for when he came out he was as "white as a sheet" and profoundly moved. When an aide asked him whether he had witnessed anything mysterious, Bonaparte would not comment and added in a gentler voice that he never wanted the incident to be spoken of again.

We seem to be touching on the realm of the occult. That happens to be my field of specialization, that is, treating it as one facet of parapsychology as a whole. Let me tell you something that might fall into that category, coming to my notice in my studies of the pyramids. Not far from the cluster of pyramids at Gizeh there is what is called the Step Pyramid of Saqqara, visible in the distance to the west.

In June, 1954, a tomb was discovered in that area which had the distinction of never having been robbed. That was clear from the fact that thieves always leave telltale signs of their having broken into the burial chamber. In this case everything in the chamber was intact. Also, more significantly, a chest containing a considerable quantity of gold and jewels lay beside the sarcophagus. As for the sarcophagus itself, it was the usual heavy granite container hewn out of solid stone. And it had a sliding lid very firmly cemented into place—not the customary slab that could be lifted directly off. When the lid was loosened, the dramatic moment arrived. As the pulleys slid the heavy cover from the sarcophagus it was completely empty! If I did not think you would laugh, I might suggest that we are here in the presence of the phenomenon of "dematerialization." Too far out? No further than some theories you might like to toy with to explain the mystery of the pyramids themselves.

The religions of ancient Egypt claimed my special attention. Considering these, one great question recurs: What was the purpose of the elaborate mummification practiced by those who could afford it, and the entombment of the body in what were hoped to be impregnable burying-places in the body of gigantic artificial mounds? There appear to be two hazards to an explanation. The first is that the pharaohs believed that some day they would return to these preserved remains, reoccupy them, and rise again for another life on earth. The other, found at a different period in the religious evolution of ancient Egypt, is to the effect that the deceased, now in his spiritual or astral body in a higher realm, could expect his immortality to last only as long as his physical remains were kept inviolate. Should disintegration or mutilation happen to the latter, his astral body, conceived as an exact replica of the physical, though of a higher "frequency," would also disintegrate and bring about his total dissolution. Did the average man, then, have to settle for a very brief spell in Hades (the "place of the dead") because he could not afford the means of prolonging his post-mortal existence?

The groups of tourists we met over the years included many who were mainly attracted to the pyramids of Gizeh and their supposed mystical elements. Among them were members of the secret society of Rosicrucians, whose reputed founder, a German knight, Christian Rosenkrantz, was an adept in Oriental magic, Arabic philosophy, and the Cabala. Besides standing in great awe of the structures at Gizeh, Rosicrucians had another interest. It was to travel to the oasis of the Fayum, some forty miles from Cairo, and there walk the shores of the lake in search of a peculiar little red flower, something like the scarlet pimpernel, to be found only in that spot. Just what mystical significance it had for them I was never able to find out.

Members of various ancient Masonic fraternities often came to our headquarters to look over our bookstore on one of the main streets in town. Not being a Mason, I could not venture to engage them in more than idle conversation. But the Great Pyramid of Cheops held a special attraction for them because of the skills of its ancient stoneworkers, as well as the fact that the pyramids had outlived the Temple of Solomon, with whom, I understand, Masons claim kinship.

Many of the founders of the United States government were Masons, and it is claimed that they received aid from a secret and august body in Europe "in establishing the United States for a peculiar and particular purpose known only to the initiated few." The Great Seal was the signature of this exalted body, and the unfinished pyramid on its reverse side sets forth symbolically the task to the accomplishment of which the United States government was dedicated from the day of its inception. It is not for me to say whether "the exalted body" referred to claimed some lineal heritage from the builders of the Great Pyramid, but the thought does come to mind. At any rate, the practice of claiming or hinting at membership in "The August Body" has been fairly common. The list of self-proclaimed initiates is said to include Sophocles, Solon, Plato, Cicero, Heraclitus, Pindar, and Pythagoras.

Far outnumbering all other visitors were latter-day adherents of the biblical "prophetic school." They usually belonged to some fundamentalist type of church and were persuaded that the Great Pyramid of Cheops embodied in its passages and chambers a host of measurements, which not only indicated important turning-points in the past but reached out into the ages to come with patent "signs of the times." Their voluminous and meticulous reasonings based on actual or supposed angles and measurements in the pyramid cannot engage us here.

But the seriousness of it all may be relieved by a true story which I heard among our Egyptologists at the embassy. One of our experts went off to take another look at the interior passages of the Pyramid of Cheops. When he was at some distance from the outside entrance, he heard a faint tapping sound. Following this up, he finally traced it to the King's Chamber itself. Imagine his astonishment at finding a man there all alone, chipping away at one of the cornerstones with mallet and chisel! He had brought a measuring tape with him and, not satisfied with the prophetic qualities of a particular measurement, was making sure that it conformed to the "sure prophecy!"

This may be the place to speak of the philosophy and religious concepts that underlay the pyramids, as far as we can decipher them with the help of scholars. I have had a life-long interest in comparative religion, and even before I reached the banks of the Nile I began studying the whole matter as affecting one's conclusions about the pyramids, of which the most important are the Gizeh complex. There is also a string of lesser pyramids stretching all the way along the left bank of the river to the Sudan. The more important of these are the Saqqara (Step) Pyramid and those at Dashur and Meidum. But the Gizeh collection are by far the most intriguing.

I believe it is safe to say that the Pyramid of Cheops, in particular, played a vital role in the religious practices and beliefs of the Pharaonic period. Unfortunately, information concerning ancient Egyptian religion is abundant but difficult to unravel. Only scattered segments of Egyptian religious history are known; the development of religious concepts was rapid, compared with that in most cultures. Whole periods are still in the dark. What we do know is that Egypt's religious beliefs, somewhat on a parallel with Hinduism in India, were riddled with confusion and inconsistency. Many gods and goddesses seem to be identical and yet they existed together. Various myths concerning the creation of the world were accepted without question. There also was much confusion in the attributes given to the gods in various contiguous localities, all of which defies attempts by scholars to compose an orderly and consistent picture.

Discovery of the Rosetta Stone in 1799 by Champollion in the Nile Delta proved to be the giant step forward in deciphering the hieroglyphs throughout Egypt, though the key thus afforded Egyptologists was not 100 percent useful; ever after the discovery of the Rosetta Stone there was much confusion in interpreting hieroglyphic records. One scholar showed me the three symbols in a cartouche and demonstrated how these could legitimately produce three different names!

The religious process seems to have begun with the worship of animals. The earliest tribes in pre-Pharaonic times each venerated their own gods, each identified with a particular animal, such as the cat at Bubastis, near modern Zagazig in the Nile Delta. There was also the Apis bull at Memphis, at the apex of the delta twelve miles from Cairo.

As civilization advanced, deities were gradually humanized. Some had the bodies of men but retained animal heads. The wolf became the god of war, and the ibis, Thoth, became the patron of learning and the arts. But then again the baboon and later the moon came to represent him. We are left to guess how these associations came about.

The cosmology of the Egyptians was both primitive and advanced. On the one hand, the common man was led to believe the earth was a disk, in which the level plains of Egypt were the center and the mountains of contiguous foreign lands round about were the rim of the disk and that which supported it—above what? The notion was that without that support the world would sink into the abysmal waters of the underworld. And it was a marked step forward in the New Kingdom (the uniting of Upper and Lower Egypt) when it was held that the divine *thought* of PTAH shaped the universe, thus anticipating, in form at least, a concept which is held by some philosophers of our own day. Said Sir James Jeans, "We are led ultimately to believe that the universe is a great thought rather than a great machine."

This monotheistic interpretation of the cosmos prevailed in Egypt only for a brief period during the reign of Ikhnaton, to be followed immediately by a reversion to polytheism. From a small handful of new gods, such as Osiris, Isis, and Horus, there emerged the awesome and dominant figure of Ra, the great Sun-God, whose symbol was the pyramid. From that time on, the pyramid became the design of the monumental tombs of the Egyptian kings, or so they were designated by most but not all scholars. By the Nineteenth Dynasty, Ra was united with the other most prominent Egyptian deity, Amon, to be known as the almighty Amon-Ra, Lord of the Worlds. But the common man never felt any close personal

tie with his gods; he was entirely dependent on the priesthood, who in turn claimed the reigning monarch as the chan-
nel of divine wisdom. Just how these ancient gods came into
being is still not fully known. It may be explained in two
ways. The monarch, after his death and ascent to the world
of eternity, would be deified. Or other individuals, who had
by long and arduous training and discipline in the spiritual
practices and knowledge of the day become worthy of initiation into the secrets of the cosmos, were venerated during
the remainder of their lives and worshipped after their de-
mise.

I would assume that in Egypt, as in other cultures, groups
of seekers practicing a spiritistic approach to the world of discarnates, came to admire certain other-worldly communicators for their superior wisdom and decided they were worthy
objects of worship. As we learn from the *Egyptian Book of
the Dead,* there was universal belief in the afterlife. The
dead were provided with food and drink, weapons, toilet
articles, and even with a funerary boat by which to make
their way to the shores of the land of spirits. Very shortly
after we left Egypt, their archaeologists discovered a large
tomb in the very shadow of the Great Pyramid. (There is
more than a theory that kings were initiated into heaven's
hierarchy in a sort of requiem mass but were actually buried
in tombs, called mastabas, close by the pyramids.) In that
particular tomb was found, among other things of great
value, a sizable wooden boat, elegant and extremely well put
together. This has prompted several historians to point out
that Heyerdahl, the intrepid Norwegian, was not correct in
assuming the ancient Egyptians made sea voyages in vessels
made of papyrus reeds strapped together. Such craft, it is
now maintained, were intended only for inland waterways;
solid wooden vessels were required for sailing the open seas
as the early Phoenicians amply demonstrated in their far-
flung voyages.

The philosophy that underlay the provision of food, weapons, and so on may not have been, shall we say, as childish as
it appears. They did not actually expect their dead to con-
sume the food or to pick up the weapons and tools for use in
the netherworld, just as Muslims today know full well that
the food they place at the graves of their loved ones in the
City of the Dead outside Cairo is never touched.

One of the findings of psychic research today is that every
person has at least two bodies, a physical entity and a nor-

material counterpart called the astral body or, by some, the etheric body. This is deemed to be an exact replica of the physical body and may well be the vehicle of the soul or spirit in an afterlife. All material objects also are supposed to have their ethereal counterparts in a range of frequencies placing them outside the laws of physics. The spirit of the person who has passed into a nonmaterial world may thus make use of, or at least take note of with gratitude, the astral counterparts of the physical objects provided for them. At any rate, that might well be the rationale of the custom.

That idea can be extended to include the mummified body of a royal personage. As long as the general form of the body was preserved, the astral counterpart would be a viable instrument in the world of spirit.

Here again we are faced with an Egyptian contradiction. As we observed, it was held that the spiritual body and the spirit of the deceased would enjoy survival of death only so long as the physical body remained intact. But the belief was also prevalent that mummification must be used to prevent reincarnation. The process was gruesome. Through the nostrils the contents of the head were extracted, and likewise all the viscera were drawn out through the anal aperture. A new life in the flesh was not possible, and so the deceased would be forced to make the best of his post-mortal condition of existence. Evidently, return by way of a mother's womb was not considered.

Still in the mystical area is a close connection between the Great Pyramid and the Egyptian mystery religions. Initiates into such systems were chosen from among those who could demonstrate their sincerity and capacity to receive the secrets of life and death. They had to undergo a long period of training and trials. Only then would the adepts receive them as aspirants to initiation. As part of their newly imparted wisdom, the great laws of the cosmos and the principles of man's relation thereto were conveyed to them on the strict understanding that they would not divulge these matters to the common folk, who were considered incapable of rising above the level of an external world of things and the satisfaction of bodily appetites.

Many, including myself, favor the idea that the secret chambers of the pyramids, many of which have probably not been discovered yet, were a kind of Holy of Holies, used, not as tombs, but as temples of initiation for aspirants of royal blood. The very highest degree of initiation would be performed in the so-called King's Chamber in the Great Pyramid. Kings were held to be almost divine anyway, and the only individuals who qualified for this most sacred rite, made all the more so by being celebrated at the heart of the Great Pyramid. The interesting thing is that this elevation or apotheosis was in order shortly after the death of the monarch, if it was not administered prior to his death.

His august departure was taken through the portals of the most perfect temple of all—perhaps a place frequently visited by Amon-Ra himself. As William Kingsland has observed, the pyramid was no mere pile of stones, but was itself an embodiment of the most important sciences, geometry and numbers. These two were the "perfect" sciences, for they dealt in exactitude, of which the spiritual counterparts were justice and truth. It was fitting that these indispensable tools of knowledge should be worked into the temple of initiation.

In addition to the astronomical relationships of the Great Pyramid it was held that these in turn were the basis of astrology, which, Kingsland points out, was "a profoundly esoteric science speaking of the great cycles of man's evolution and understood only by the adepts."

According to another lifelong student of the subject, Manly P. Hall, "the illumined of antiquity passed through the mystic passageways and chambers of the Great Pyramid, entering as mortals—albeit highly instructed mortals—to emerge as gods."

"The candidate," says Hall, "was laid in the great stone coffer, which stood empty and uncovered as a symbol of resurrection, and for three days his spirit, freed from its mortal clay, wandered near the portals of eternity. His *ka*, or astral double, flew birdlike through the spiritual spheres of space, and he discovered that all the universe was a manifestation of life; all was progress; all was eternal growth and evolution. He realized that his body was a home which he could slip out of and return to without dying. Thus he achieved true immortality. At the end of three days he returned to himself again. Having personally experienced the great mystery, he was a true initiate—one who beheld, and one to whom religion had fulfilled her duty by bringing him to the light of God."

Such, then, was the controlled astral journey which the initiate was enabled to make, not at all at variance with the reports given us by those who have been able to project themselves into higher spheres, or who slip into that transcendent state of consciousness unawares. Would we not be justified in surmising that the empty coffers in the Great Pyramid and others were a kind of baptismal font? In this the postulant was laid and was born again, now to be revered as an adept or as a god.

Brunes, the Danish mathematician and philosopher, tells us that during the initiation ceremony the candidate was placed in the coffer and, by the ministrations of the chief priest, was put into a deep trance symbolizing death itself. He awoke from that condition recalling that he "had wandered in the world of the gods," or discarnates. He was regarded as having been reborn.

You can see how much this recalls what we read today in the literature of psychic research. In fact, Henri Furville in *La Science Secrète* claims that the texts of the Book of the Dead and indeed certain passages of the New Testament are incomprehensible to those who do not study them from the point of view of parapsychology. The baffling texts, he says, "shine in the light of initiation, and the practices which seem extraordinary and even absurd to the uninformed, are, on the contrary, the result of a most profound science." Personally, I favor the idea that the secret chambers of the pyramids were shrines or temples of initiation, not tombs meant to give eternal shelter to the bodies of deceased pharaohs. It is noteworthy that the chambers are bare of hieroglyphs, thus not being identified with any particular person. True, the hieroglyphs of Cheops's name, somewhat crudely drawn in red paint, not chiseled, are not found in the chamber itself, but in one of the almost inaccessible crevices between horizontal slabs of stone placed outside and above the chamber to take the weight off the ceiling. It was almost as though they were never meant to be found. The heavy lids of the coffers may well have been replaced after each of the seldom-held initiation ceremonies, but the coffers were always found empty even in chambers at the heart of pyramids that had never been robbed!

To conclude the account of my personal odyssey, let me recall that, in the course of our wartime work at the British embassy we brought together members of the Allied forces on leave in Cairo for entertainment and a chance to meet our Egyptian friends. Among them were Noel Coward and the fabulous Josephine Baker. Wearing a smart French Air Force uniform, and with her inimitable spotlight manner, Josephine brought the house down, although suffering from a cold.

Of course, these visiting celebrities were not allowed to go on their way without a visit to the pyramids. This was often done late in the afternoon, when most of the tourist traffic had moved out of the way; and that would be followed by dinner within sight of Cheops and his neighbors.

Now, let us turn to what the French call *Le sortilège des pyramides*—the mystical charm or wizardry of those timeless monuments.

Today's tourists are treated to an added attraction at the site. It is called "Son et Lumière," which combines sound, light and music to revive ancient history. This reenactment is extremely well done both in conception and execution; the show, put on every evening shortly after sunset, is most captivating. Coordinated sweeps of colored floodlights illuminate the noble Cheops against the blackness of the sky, and the stabbing beam transfixes the Sphinx from time to time. All this is accompanied by the exotic sounds of ancient instruments and the voices of actors, leaving an impression never to be forgotten. (The visitor should watch the daily papers to see in which of four languages the show is being presented that evening. These are English, French, German and Arabic.)

The pyramids by moonlight is another moving experience. At that latitude a full moon lights up the scene with almost daylight brilliance. Small parties of tourists often take advantage of the camps in the vicinity and stay overnight just to enjoy the exotic surroundings under the moon.

Every now and then groups of friends and myself would drive out to that site, eat supper under the moon and sleep out on the sand near the pyramids. That was in the earlier years of our stay in Egypt. It was all very proper, mind you. We were well chaperoned. One had to be careful of two things: to watch out for scorpions, and to cover one's head before going to sleep, for the dew fell almost like rain during the night and the sand around us would be quite wet in the morning.

I had the good fortune to become acquainted with a charming American young lady in Cairo; and there came a time when we felt that the pyramids would add a touch of romance to *our* romance! They surely did.

It was the occasion of a moonlight picnic to Gizeh with a few friends. We consumed our meal hard by the mighty

Cheops. And as the others began to drift away on the path to the Sphinx, we slipped off in another direction and sat spell-bound in a secluded spot surveying the moonlit scene—well, not exactly. We were naturally more interested in the sight of each other and, as we had become more than the best of friends by that time, we pledged our troth—with an added sense of romance that seemed to pervade the supercharged surroundings.

We have shared this secret with very few and can add that the marriage that was placed in the cards that evening under the Gizeh moon has—after the lapse of more than forty years—proved to have been the best of all ventures. If the shade of Nefertiti was there that evening, attempting to divert my attention, she must have realized that she did not have a chance!

Literature of the
Great Pyramid

by Martin Gardner

Mr. Gardner, as has been noted in the Introduction to this volume, is a well-informed and often witty critic of the pseudo-supernatural. His book, Fads and Fallacies in the Name of Science, *from which this chapter is taken, ranges from the hollow-earth hypothesis to food faddism. Martin Gardner conducts the "Mathematical Games" column in* Scientific American. *His most recent book is* Mathematical Carnival *(1975). The following survey of the literature of the Great Pyramid deals with research and ideas that were prominent in the late nineteenth century but continue to have an impact in our own time.*

> The Great, the Mighty God, the Lord of Hosts . . . which hast set signs and wonders in the land of Egypt, even unto this day. . . .
>
> —*Jeremiah* 32:18-20

The literature of biblical archaeology presents a bewildering panorama. It ranges all the way from competent, objective studies by men who took great pains not to draw unwarranted inferences from their artifacts, to the work of men who have twisted their material in every conceivable way to make it conform to biblical records. Thousands of books and pamphlets have been written in the past hundred years to show that the "latest findings" of archaeology confirm all the details of scriptural history—especially the miracle stories at which unbelievers scoff. In some cases, it is hard to believe the distortion has been unconscious. Professor Hubert Grimme, for example, of the University of Munich, published in the twenties a "translation" of a stone tablet which told how the infant Moses had been rescued from the bulrushes by Pharaoh's daughter. It later came to light that the professor had made free use of cracks and weather marks on the stone, combining them with the hieroglyphics to make the translation come out right.

In English, the most dignified books in this pseudo-archaeological literature are by Sir Charles Martson—*The Bible Is True*, 1934; *New Bible Evidence*, 1934; and *The Bible Comes Alive*, 1937. Among the less scholarly, John O. Kinnaman's *Diggers for Facts*, 1940, is a good recent example. From it you will learn that Abraham's home and even his signature have been unearthed, as well as evidence that St. Paul once preached in England. Kinnaman is cautious, however, about identifying the salty remains of Lot's wife. "There are many actual pillars of salt in that region," he writes, "but which may be the remains of the unfortunate woman, no one can tell."

Expeditions to Mount Ararat, to find Noah's Ark, take place every few years. Egerton Sykes, head of the Hörbiger Institute in England and editor of an Atlantis magazine, planned such an expedition a few years ago, but Russian authorities put pressure on the Ottoman officials at Ankara, and he was refused a visa. According to the Russians, his expedition was part of an "Anglo-American military plot to spy on the Russian borders in sight of Ararat." However, in 1949 another expedition, led by Dr. Aaron Smith, of Greensboro, N.C., did manage to climb 12,000 feet up the side of Ararat. Unfortunately, they failed to find the Ark. "We can't say if the Ark may have landed at a lower level," Smith reported, "or if it was completely buried by the debris of earthquakes, violent in this region. Again, it may exist on the north side of the range, under ice and snow. We have not found it; but we sure have cleared the way for others who may have better luck than we had."

It would be impossible, of course, to survey even briefly the literature of eccentric biblical archaeology. One aspect, however, known as Pyramidology, is sufficiently curious and colorful to warrant special attention. With this topic (which rivals Atlantis in the number of books devoted to it) the remainder of the chapter will be concerned.

The Great Pyramid of Egypt was involved in many medieval and Renaissance cults, especially in the Rosicrucian and other occult traditions, but it was not until 1859 that modern Pyramidology was born. This was the year that John

Taylor, an eccentric partner in a London publishing firm, issued his *The Great Pyramid: Why Was It Built? And Who Built It?*

Taylor never visited the Pyramid, but the more he studied its structure, the more he became convinced that its architect was not an Egyptian, but an Israelite acting under divine orders. Perhaps it was Noah himself. "He who built the ark was, of all men, the most competent to direct the building of the Great Pyramid," Taylor wrote. The picture is rather amusing, of poor old Noah, after his Herculean task of building the Ark and surviving the Deluge, being sent to Egypt to direct the even more Herculean labor of building the Pyramid!

Taylor's chief reason for thinking the Pyramid part of God's plan was the fact that he found in its structure all kinds of mathematical truths which far surpassed the knowledge of ancient Egypt. For example, if you divide the monument's height into twice the side of its base, you obtain a fairly close approximation of *pi* (the ratio of diameter to circumference of a circle). In addition, Taylor found elaborate reasons for thinking that the measuring unit used by the Pyramid's architect was none other than the biblical "cubit" employed by Noah in the construction of the Ark, by Abraham in building the Tabernacle, and by Solomon in the architecture of his temples. The "sacred cubit" was, Taylor thought, about twenty-five inches, and based on the length of the earth's axis. Since the earth's diameter varies considerably, because of the flattening at the poles, what could be a more natural basis for a divine unit than the axis on which our globe rotates? If you divide the axis by 400,000, you obtain the sacred cubit. Taylor found other divine units of measurement in the Pyramid—in the capacity of a granite coffer in the King's Chamber, for example—all of which he thought had bases in nature and were therefore superior to those of other measuring systems.

In addition to all the supposed truths embodied in the Pyramid, Taylor also found a score of passages in both the *Old* and *New Testament* which, if wrenched from their contexts, can be interpreted as references to the stone monument. For example, we read in *Isaiah* 19:19-20: "In that day shall there be an altar to the Lord in the midst of the land of Egypt . . . and it shall be for a sign and for a witness unto the Lord of hosts. . . ." And in *Job* 38:5-7: "Who hath laid the measures thereof, if thou knowest? Or who hath stretched the line upon it? Whereupon are the foundations thereof fastened? or who laid the cornerstone thereof, when the morning stars sang together, and all the sons of God shouted for joy?" Even St. Paul spoke of the Pyramid, Taylor believed, in such passages as ". . . Jesus Christ himself being the chief corner stone; in whom all the building, fitly framed together, groweth unto an holy temple of the Lord" (*Ephesians* 2:20-21). The Pyramid symbolized, he explained, the true Church with Christ as the topmost corner stone (this symbol, incidentally, has been popular in Christian mystical lore, and was adopted by the founding fathers as the reverse side of the United States Seal).

Taylor's speculation would probably have soon been forgotten had it not been for the Astronomer-Royal of Scotland, a University of Edinburgh professor named Charles Piazzi Smyth. Fired with enthusiasm for Taylor's theory, Smyth soon convinced himself there were greater truths symbolized in the Pyramid than even Taylor suspected. His 664-page work, *Our Inheritance in the Great Pyramid*, is to biblical Pyramidology what Donnelly's book is to Atlantology. The first edition, in 1864, was an immediate success. It went through four later editions (the last, greatly revised, in 1890), was translated into many languages, and has far exceeded all subsequent works on the topic in its influence. In 1865, Smyth went to Egypt at his own expense to make his own measurements of the Pyramid. The results of this research appeared in his three-volume *Life and Work at the Great Pyramid*, 1867, and *On the Antiquity of Intellectual Man*, 1868.

Our Inheritance is a classic of its kind. Few books illustrate so beautifully the ease with which an intelligent man, passionately convinced of a theory, can manipulate his subject matter in such a way as to make it conform to previously held opinions. Unfortunately, space permits only the barest résumé of Smyth's sensational findings.

To begin with, Smyth discovered that the base of the Pyramid, divided by the width of a casing stone, equaled exactly 365—the number of days in the year. Casing stones originally composed the outside surface of the monument. The first of these stones was unearthed after Taylor's death, so its width had not been known to him. The stone measured slightly more than twenty-five inches, and Smyth concluded that this length was none other than the sacred cubit. If we adopt a new inch—Smyth calls it the "Pyramid inch"—which is exactly one twenty-fifth of the width of the casing stone, then we obtain the smallest divine unit of measurement used in the monument's construction. It is exactly one ten-millionth of the earth's polar radius. Somehow, it had been passed on through the generations, the Scottish astronomer believed, until it became the Anglo-Saxon inch, but in the process altered slightly, making the British inch a trifle short of the sacred unit. Many years later a number of other casing stones were dug up. They had entirely different widths. By that time, however, the Pyramid inch had become so firmly established in the literature of Pyramidology that devotees merely shrugged and admitted that the first casing stone just "happened" to be a cubit wide.

With incredible zeal, Smyth applied his Pyramid inch to every measurable portion of the Pyramid, inside and out, to see how many scientific and historical truths he could discover. These he found in great profusion. For example, when the height of the Pyramid is multiplied by ten to the ninth power, you obtain a distance which approximates the distance from the earth to the sun. Similar manipulations of Pyramid lengths give you the earth's mean density, the period of precession of its axis, the mean temperature of the earth's surface, and many other scientific facts only discovered in recent times. In addition to a system of sacred measuring units for length, weight, volume, and so on, Smyth even proposed a "Pyramid thermometer." It used freezing point as zero, and a fifty-degree mark based on the temperature inside the King's Chamber, which was on the fiftieth level of the monument's masonry.

Smyth's most spectacular contribution, however, was the elaboration of a theory proposed by one Robert Menzies—that there is a great outline of history symbolized by the Pyramid's internal passageways. When these passages are properly measured in Pyramid inches, counting an inch as equal to a year, and the symbolism correctly interpreted, you emerge with the principal dates in the earth's past and future. You discover, for instance, that the world was created about 4,004 years before Christ. The Flood, the time of the Exodus, and the date the Pyramid was built are also indicated. The beginning of a sloping passage called the Grand Gallery marks the birth of Christ. Other features indicate the Lord's Atonement (after thirty-three inch-years of life), his descent into Hell, and final Resurrection. Continuing upward along the gallery, one discovers that it terminates at a point between 1882 and 1911, depending on how the length of the Grand Gallery is measured. To Smyth this twenty-nine-year period is the great Tribulation which will precede the Second Coming of Christ.

It is not difficult to understand how Smyth achieved these astonishing scientific and historical correspondences. If you set about measuring a complicated structure like the Pyramid, you will quickly have on hand a great abundance of lengths to play with. If you have sufficient patience to juggle them about in various ways, you are certain to come out with many figures which coincide with important historical dates or figures in the sciences. Since you are bound by no rules, it would be odd indeed if this search for Pyramid "truths" failed to meet with considerable success.

Take the Pyramid's height, for example. Smyth multiplies it by ten to the ninth power to obtain the distance to the sun. The nine here is purely arbitrary. And if no simple multiple had yielded the distance to the sun, he could try other multiples to see if it gave the distance to the moon, or the nearest star, or any other scientific figure.

This process of juggling is rendered infinitely easier by two significant facts. (1) Measurements of various Pyramid lengths are far from established. Competent archaeologists in Smyth's day disagreed about almost all of them, including the most basic of all, the base length of the Pyramid. Later archaeologists, after Smyth, made more accurate measurements and found still different figures. In many cases Smyth had a choice of several lengths to pick from. In other cases he used measurements made by himself. And sometimes he added together conflicting measurements and used the average. (2) The figures which represent scientific truths are equally vague. The distance to the sun, for example, was not known with great accuracy in Smyth's day, and besides, the distance varies considerably because the earth's path is not a circle but an ellipse. In such cases you have a wide choice of figures. You can use the earth's shortest distance to the sun, or the longest, or the mean. And in all three cases, you can choose between conflicting estimates made by different astronomers of the time. The same ambiguity applies to almost every scientific "truth" employed by Smyth.

The only Pyramid "truth" which cannot be explained easily in terms of such juggling is the value *pi*. The Egyptians may have purposely made use of this ratio, but it seems more likely that it was a by-product of another construction.

Herodotus states that the Pyramid was built so the area of each face would equal the area of a square whose side is equal to the Pyramid's height. If such a construction is made, it fits the Pyramid perfectly, and the ratio of height to twice the base will automatically be a surprisingly accurate value for *pi*. (See *Popular Astronomy*, April, 1943, p. 185.)

Both Taylor and Smyth made a great deal of the fact that the number five is a key number in Pyramid construction. It has five corners and five sides. The Pyramid inch is one fifth of one fifth of a cubit. And so on. Joseph Seiss, one of Smyth's disciples, puts it as follows: "This intense *fiveness* could not have been accidental, and likewise corresponds with the arrangements of God, both in nature and revelation. Note the fiveness of termination to each limb of the human body, The five senses, the five books of Moses, the twice five precepts of the Decalogue."

Just for fun, if one looks up the facts about the Washington Monument in the *World Almanac*, he will find considerable fiveness. Its height is 555 feet and 5 inches. The base is 55 feet square, and the windows are set at 500 feet from the base. If the base is multiplied by 60 (or five times the number of months in a year), it gives 3,300, which is the exact weight of the capstone in pounds. Also, the word "Washington" has exactly ten letters (two times five). And if the weight of the capstone is multiplied by the base, the result is 181,500—a fairly close approximation of the speed of light in miles per second. If the base is measured with a "Monument foot," which is slightly smaller than the standard foot, its side comes to 56½ feet. This times 33,000 yields a figure even closer to the speed of light.

And is it not significant that the Monument is in the form of an *obelisk*—an ancient Egyptian structure? Or that a picture of the Great Pyramid appears on a dollar bill, on the side opposite *Washington's* portrait? Moreover, the decision to print the Pyramid (i.e., the reverse side of the United States seal) on dollar bills was announced by the Secretary of the Treasury on June 15, 1935—both date and year being multiples of five. And are there not exactly twenty-five letters (five times five) in the title, "The Secretary of the Treasury"?

It should take an average mathematician about fifty-five minutes to discover the above "truths," working only with the meager figures provided by the *Almanac*. Considering the fact that Smyth made his own measurements, obtaining hundreds of lengths with which to work, and that he spent twenty years mulling over these figures, it is not hard to see how he achieved such remarkable results.

Nevertheless, Smyth's books made a profound impression on millions of naïve readers. Dozens of volumes appeared in all languages carrying on the great work and adding additional material. In France, the leading advocate of Pyramidology was Abbé F. Moigno, Canon of St. Denis, Paris. An International Institute for Preserving and Perfecting Weights and Measures was organized in Boston, in 1879, at a meeting in Old South Church. The purpose of the Society was to work for the revision of measuring units to conform to sacred Pyramid standards, and to combat the "atheistic metrical system" of France. President James A. Garfield was a supporter of the Society, though he declined to serve as its president.

A periodical called *The International Standard* was published during the 1880's by the Ohio Auxiliary of the Society, in Cleveland. The president of the Ohio group, a civil engineer who prided himself on having an arm exactly one cubit in length, had this to say in the first issue: "We believe our work to be of God; we are actuated by no selfish or mercenary motive. We depreciate personal antagonisms of every kind, but we proclaim a ceaseless antagonism to that great evil, the French Metric System. . . . The jests of the ignorant and the ridicule of the prejudiced, fall harmless upon us and deserve no notice. . . . It is the Battle of the Standards. May our banner be ever upheld in the cause of Truth, Freedom, and Universal Brotherhood, founded upon a just weight and a just measure, which alone are acceptable to the Lord."

A later issue printed the words and music of a song, the fourth verse of which ran:

> Then down with every "metric" scheme
>   Taught by the foreign school,
> We'll worship still our Father's God!
>   And keep our Father's "rule"!
> A perfect inch, a perfect pint,
>   The Anglo's honest pound,
> Shall hold their place upon the earth,
>   Till time's last trump shall sound!

The prophetic portions of Smyth's work appealed strongly to Protestant fundamentalists of all denominations—especially in England. One of the most popular early books, *Miracle in Stone*, 1877, by Joseph Seiss, ran through fourteen editions. A Col. J. Garnier produced a book in 1905 which proved by the Pyramid that Christ would return in 1920. Walter Wynn, in 1926, issued a similar work. Undaunted by the failure of its prophecies, he wrote another book in 1933 containing equally bad predictions. Bertrand Russell, in one of his essays, summed up this literature as follows:

"I like also the men who study the Great Pyramid, with a view to deciphering its mystical lore. Many great books have been written on this subject, some of which have been presented to me by their authors. It is a singular fact that the Great Pyramid always predicts the history of the world accurately up to the date of publication of the book in question, but after that date it becomes less reliable. Generally the author expects, very soon, wars in Egypt, followed by Armageddon and the coming of the Antichrist, but by this time so many people have been recognized as Antichrist that the reader is reluctantly driven to scepticism."

An American preacher enormously impressed by Smyth's researches was Charles Tazé Russell, of Allegheny, Pa., founder of the sect now known as Jehovah's Witnesses. In 1891, Pastor Russell published the third volume of his famous series *Studies in the Scripture*. It is a book of biblical prophecy, supplemented by evidence from the Great Pyramid. A letter from Smyth is reproduced in which the Scottish astronomer praises Russell highly for his new and original contributions.

According to Russell, the Bible and Pyramid reveal clearly that the Second Coming of Christ took place invisibly in 1874. This ushered in forty years of "Harvest" during which the true members of the Church are to be called together under Russell's leadership. Before the close of 1914, the Millennium will begin. The dead will rise and be given a "second chance" to accept Christ. Those who refuse are to be annihilated, leaving the world completely cleansed of evil. Members of the church alive at the beginning of the Millennium will simply live on forever. This is the meaning of the well-known slogan of the Witnesses—"Millions now living will never die."

In England, two brothers, John and Morton Edgar, were so impressed by Russell's pyramid theories that they hurried to Egypt to make measurements of their own. There they found "beautiful confirmations" of the pastor's views "as day by day first one, and then the other, discovered fresh beauties in the symbolic and prophetic teaching of this marvellous structure." Their heroic research is recorded for posterity in two weighty tomes, from the first of which the above quotation is taken. The volumes appeared in 1910 and 1913, under the title, *The Great Pyramid Passages and Chambers*.

To the great disappointment of the Russellites, 1914 ushered in nothing more dramatic than the World War, and the sect lost thousands of members. New editions of Russell's Pyramid study were issued with the wording altered slightly at crucial spots to make the errors less obvious. Thus, a 1910 edition had read, ". . . The deliverance of the saints must take place some time before 1914. . . ." (p. 228) But in 1923, this sentence read, ". . . The deliverance of the saints must take place very soon after 1914. . . ." Morton Edgar (brother John died before the great disappointment) produced a series of booklets in the twenties which followed the then current Russellite line—namely, that in 1914 Christ (already on earth since 1874) had begun an *invisible* reign of righteousness.

Judge J. F. Rutherford, who succeeded Russell after the pastor died in 1916, eventually discarded Pyramidology entirely. Writing in the November 15 and December 1, 1928, issues of *The Watch Tower and Herald*, Rutherford releases a double-barreled blast against it, and advances many ingenious arguments that the so-called Altar in Egypt was really inspired by Satan for the purpose of misleading the faithful. Did Jesus ever mention the Pyramid? Of course not. To study it, the Judge writes, is a waste of time and indicates lack of faith in the all-sufficiency of the Bible. Whether Morton Edgar remained a faithful Witness after this date, renouncing his lifetime work on the Pyramid, would be interesting to know.

The Judge did not remind his readers in these articles that he, too, had been guilty of a prophetic error. For many years he had taught that 1925 would mark the beginning of the great jubilee year. Alas, it also had passed without perceptible upheavals. The sect now discourages the sale and reading of Russell's writings, and although members still believe the Millennium is about to dawn, no definite dates are set.

Another fundamentalist sect that has made even stronger use of the "Bible in Stone," is the Anglo-Israel movement. This cult regards the Anglo-Saxon and Celtic peoples as descendents of the ten lost tribes of Israel, and therefore heir to all the promises God made to Abraham. In the United States, the leading organization is the Anglo-Saxon Federation of America, with headquarters at Haverhill, Mass. Their handsome monthly magazine, *Destiny*, has been going now for more than twenty years.

Anglo-Israel's outstanding Pyramid work is a monumental tome, the size of a volume of the *Encyclopaedia Britannica*, called *The Great Pyramid: Its Divine Message*. It was written by David Davidson, a structural engineer in Leeds, England, and first published in 1924. A revised eighth edition appeared in 1940. The book is based on Smyth, with important differences in the prophetic section. The "Final Tribulation" of the Anglo-Saxon peoples was to begin in 1928 and extend to 1936. From September 16, 1936, until August 20, 1953, the Anglo-Saxons—i.e., the "true" Israel—will be brought together and given divine protection against a coalition of world powers seeking to destroy them. This will be the Armageddon period, terminated by the return of Christ.

Numerous Anglo-Israel books and pamphlets have been based on Davidson's work, notably the books of Basil Stewart. In the United States, the Haverhill group is currently selling the tenth edition of *Great Pyramid Proof of God*, by George F. Riffert, of Easton, Pa. It likewise is a popular version of Davidson. The first edition, which appeared in 1932, placed great stress on the September 16, 1936, date. There was, in fact, considerable excitement among Anglo-Israelites in both England and the United States when this day approached, but it slipped by without visible cataclysms.

The present edition of Riffert's book has an added chapter in which the author confesses, "A very real problem was, and still is, to ascertain the literal significance and character of the epoch whose crisis date was September 16, 1936." He suggests several events which took place on that day, the most important of which was "that the Duke of Windsor, then King of England, notified his prime minister, Mr. Baldwin, of his determination to marry Mrs. Simpson."

Riffert concludes: ". . . By 1953 the present Babylon-Beast-Gentile type of Civilization, the Capitalistic System of Money profits by exploitation and usury, the Armageddon Conflict, the Resurrection and Translation of God's spiritual Israel preparatory to their administrative service in the New Social or Economic Order, the overthrow of dictatorships, the regeneration and transformation of the Anglo-Saxon Nations into the worldwide Kingdom of God, and literal return of Jesus Christ as King of Kings to prepare and perpetuate the Millennial Age, will all have come to pass."

Adventist sects have a distressing habit of refusing to blow away when one of their major prophecies fails. It is too easy to discover "errors" in calculations and make appropriate revisions. Nevertheless, it will be interesting to observe the mental gyrations of the Haverhill leaders after August 20, 1953 slips by.

It is perhaps worth mentioning that there is also a vast occult literature dealing with the Pyramid—especially in Rosicrucian and theosophical traditions. The biblical prophecies of Smyth are rejected, but the authors find in the monument a great deal of mathematical, scientific, astrological, and occult symbolism which varies widely with individual writers. According to Madame Blavatsky, the interior of the Pyramid was used for the performance of sacred rituals connected with the Egyptian *Book of the Dead,* and most theosophists today assume there are vast mysteries of some sort connected with the stone monument that are known only to initiates. The best reference on this approach is a two-volume work by British theosophist William Kingland, *Great Pyramid in Fact and in Theory,* 1932-35. Another occult approach, connecting the Pyramid with the mystical Jewish writings known as the Cabala, will be found in J. Ralston Skinner's *Key to the Hebrew-Egyptian Mystery,* 1875 (revised in 1931).

As worthless as all this literature is, it is not entirely worthless if we can see in it an important object lesson. No book has ever demonstrated more clearly than Smyth's (the other Pyramid books, of course, to a lesser degree) how easy it is to work over an undigested mass of data and emerge with a pattern, which at first glance, is so intricately put together that it is difficult to believe it is nothing more than the product of a man's brain. In a sense, this is true of almost all the books of pseudo-scientists. In one way or another, they do not let the data speak for themselves. Consciously or unconsciously, their preconceived dogmas twist and mold the objective facts into forms which support the dogmas, but have no basis in the exterior world. Sir Flinders Petrie, a famous archaeologist who made some highly exact Pyramid measurements, reports that he once caught a Pyramidologist secretly filing down a projecting stone to make it conform to one of his theories!

Perhaps this tendency to distort data operates in its subtlest forms in the great cyclical theories of history—the works of men like Hegel, Spengler, Marx, and perhaps, though one must say it in hushed tones, the works of Toynbee. The ability of the mind to fool itself by an unconscious "fudging" on the facts—an overemphasis here and underemphasis there—is far greater than most people realize. The literature of Pyramidology stands as a permanent and pathetic tribute to that ability.

Will the work of the prophetic historians mentioned above seem to readers of the year 2,000 as artificial in their constructions as the predictions of the Pyramidologists? Chesterton's hilarious fantasy of the future, *Napoleon of Notting Hill* (which opens, by the way, like Orwell's novel, in 1984) begins with these wise words:

"The human race, to which so many of my readers belong, has been playing at children's games from the beginning . . . and one of the games to which it is most attached is called, 'Keep to-morrow dark,' and which is also named (by the rustics in Shropshire, I have no doubt) 'Cheat the Prophet.' The players listen very carefully and respectfully to all that the clever men have to say about what is to happen in the next generation. The players then wait until all the clever men are dead, and bury them nicely. They then go and do something else. That is all. For a race of simple tastes, however, it is great fun."

Experiments in Pyramid Power

by James Raymond Wolfe

Mr. Wolfe, who describes his personal efforts to harness pyramid power, is a lifetime student of paranormal phenomena. He was educated at Loyola University and Johns Hopkins University and has been Clark University Lecturer in Paranormal Phenomena. James Raymond Wolfe, it will be noted, did not undertake any experiments in the area of sharpening razor blades; asked why this type of experiment was missing from his manuscript, he said that he "did not find them promising" and had "felt no particular motivation in this direction." The author feels that more extensive research is required before even his own experiments may be regarded as definitive or validated.

For the past twenty-four hours I have been carefully monitoring my visceral sensations for evidences of an attack of botulism. Yesterday at noon I ate a strip of beef which had lain for ten days at room temperature unprotected by anything more than a pyramidal structure of bristol board.

The beef had become dark and dry to the point of brittleness. It resembled a piece of "jerky," meat preserved by the primitive method of slicing and drying in bright sunlight. The flavor was similar, too: not unpleasant but rather glutinous.

A control piece of beef, kept under an inverted cardboard box, decayed, becoming moldy and malodorous. At the reiterated suggestion of the lady who cares for my apartment, it was discarded halfway through the experiment.

Anyhow, *B. Clostridium botulinum* failed to make his presence felt, and it would appear that he was either defunct or debilitated in the strip of meat I ate. This inclines me to agree with those who assert that animal protein can be preserved in an edible state by storage in a pyramidal shell of cardboard.

That beef experiment was the latest in a somewhat desultory program conducted over the past year and a half. Its purpose was to research reports of unusual manifestations of energy that seem to depend upon geometrical form rather than substance. A number of those experiments will be detailed below and an attempt will be made to show how they suggest the nature of the energy involved. At this point, however, it seems useful to set forth certain pertinent background information.

From time to time, travelers in Egypt have remarked about certain perceptual experiences they have had in connection with the Great Pyramid of Gizeh. Some claimed that they saw an emanation of pale blue light radiating from its top. Others said they felt an exhilaration, as of energy flowing through them, when they stood at its summit. And of course there have been those who claim that, while in its interior, they were selected by preternatural guides to be instructed in mysteries which they may divulge under no conditions less than the receipt of a magazine coupon and a respectable fee.

But, setting those things aside, we find that almost fifty years ago, a French traveler, Antoine Bovis, was successful in experimental verification of an extraordinary observation he made in the King's Chamber of the pyramid. In the chamber he found a number of refuse cans containing the swept-up bodies of cats, rats, and mice that had wandered into the pyramid and died there. He was surprised to find that no odor came from the dead animals, all of which seemed to be in a mummified condition.

His curiosity piqued, upon his return home Bovis constructed a cardboard pyramid shell accurately scaled down from the dimensions of the Gizeh structure. He put a dead cat in it at an elevation equivalent to that of the King's Chamber in the original. The cat did not decay, but instead desiccated into a mummy. Bovis got similar results in subsequent experiments with other animals, birds, and fish.

In the 1950's, in Czechoslovakia, radio engineer Karel Drbal began to look into the Bovis experiments. He claimed a discovery of his own: used safety razor blades stored in cardboard pyramids regained their sharpness. In 1959 he applied for and obtained Czech Patent 91304 for his Cheops Pyramid Razor Blade Sharpener.

Drbal's Sharpener attracted the attention of psychic buffs all over the world and this led to the designing of a number of experiments, few of which were ever proclaimed unsuccessful. Along with blade sharpening and mummification of plant and animal tissue, these included the removal of tarnish from silver; improvement in the taste of coffee, wine, water, fruit juice, and tobacco; increase in the rate of plant growth and the healing of wounds; the relief of headaches by wearing pyramidal hats of aluminum foil; and the use of pyramid-treated water as a digestive aid and a face lotion. Some experimenters claimed to be especially benefited by meditating in a pyramid. And naturally there were a host of claims of extraordinarily developed ESP.

The concurrence of so many experimenters in testifying to such effects tends to invite participation in the game. Accordingly, I began to construct a number of bristol board pyramids of various sizes.

The Gizeh Pyramid is quite apparently constructed on functions of *pi*, the ratio of the circumference of a circle to its diameter, roughly 3.14. The way this works out is that if you want a pyramid two feet high, then it should have a base 3.14 feet long to be in the same proportion as the Gizeh structure. Later we'll see an implication in this; right now we want to simplify the pyramid building.

You can make things easier for yourself—assuming you want to build a pyramid—by using the metric system. Then the following basic proportions apply:

1,000	millimeter	height
1,495	millimeter	side
1,571	millimeter	base

By *side*, I mean the length of the line where two faces of the pyramid join. For a pyramid of any given size, those proportions must be maintained. Whatever height is selected can be considered as a unit. Then the base is 1.571 times that unit and a side, 1.495 times. You'll find it convenient to cut out the four side triangles and lay them on a flat surface so that three sets of edges meet. Tape those with any kind of tape you have handy. Erect the pyramid so that the fourth set of edges meet and tape them together.

Inside the pyramid it is useful to have a platform or support with a top, on which you can position things at one third the distance from base to apex, the approximate location of the King's Chamber.

The first experiment I did was with some cheap supermarket hamburger. In New York this is permitted to contain as much as 25 percent fat, something that becomes obvious as soon as you handle it. It spoils fast, an advantage in checking the progress of the experiment with minimal delay.

I used a pyramid of 150 millimeters height—just a hair under six inches—and a rectangular cardboard box which I made of the same material as the pyramid, bristol board. It was of the same height and had the same base measurement, 236 millimeters. Two-inch demitasse cups served as platforms in each, inverted, of course.

I determined a true north-south line by plotting several sextant observations of the sun and determining the azimuth at which it held the highest altitude. Both box and pyramid were aligned with a side along that line. A teaspoonful of hamburger was placed on each platform and covered by the pyramid and box, respectively.

At the end of forty-eight hours the sample under the box was quite obviously spoiled. That under the pyramid had darkened and its surface was dry in appearance; however, it gave no sign of spoilage. The control sample was disposed of. At the end of ten days, the pyramid sample had shrunk and become quite dry, though with a rather soapy feeling. It was odorless. I did not taste it.

I boiled some of the uncooked hamburger in a quantity of water, defatted it in the refrigerator, and used it with some commercial unflavored gelatine to make a nutrient base for bacterial culture.

The broth was poured into a common dessert dish and allowed to jell, being covered all the time with a sheet of glass. The edge of the dish was Vaselined to facilitate its juncture with the glass and keep out air. Crumbled specimens of the pyramid meat sample were placed on the surface of the broth. The whole was stored at room temperature. In forty-eight hours minute cultures of bacteria were evident. Their pattern could not be said to conform to the distribution pattern of the meat pieces. I conclude that bacteria entered through air contamination during the setting up of the experiment, but must concede that better control is needed.

I repeated the first part of the experiment using two cherry tomatoes (*Lycopersicon esculentum cerasiform*) of similar color and firmness. I washed each in tap water and placed them upon the sterilized cup bottoms in pyramid and control box. In ten days, the control specimen was mottled with brown and showed considerable mold. The pyramid tomato had shriveled but retained its bright red color. On dissection it revealed no sign of decay.

Experiments in connection with seed germination presented a problem. For one thing, it is dark inside a pyramid and this prevents the development of chlorophyl, without which no plant is going to get very far. Another factor is the suppression of new growth which is implied by the lack of bacteria in the pyramid meat samples. Some experimenters have reported that it is possible to "charge" aluminum foil in a pyramid for six weeks and achieve a speeded-up seed germination in potting soil placed on top of it. It seemed to me that it might be interesting to borrow a trick from atomic physics and use carbon rods to absorb the pyramid charge.

From an art store I obtained two 6-B graphite sticks. For a period of two weeks, one reposed in the control box and another in a pyramid. Both were oriented with their long axes north to south. I obtained some unhusked sunflower seeds from a store that sells them for home-growing to natural food enthusiasts, and I got some potting soil from a florist. The potting soil was placed to a depth of 40 millimeters in each of two square Pyrex baking dishes. Concentric furrows were grooved in each soil surface with the point of a pencil. Seeds which had been soaked in water for eight hours (retailer's instructions) were distributed in each set of furrows. In the center of one dish the pyramid-charged rod was placed and the control rod was placed in the center of the other.

Germination became apparent around the charged rod in slightly less than twenty-four hours. Its progress was from the rod toward the edge of the tray. This was quite marked. Germination in the control tray showed a random distribution. By the end of the week, the growth of the plants in the tray with the charged rod showed a height averaging about 70 millimeters in the immediate vicinity of the rod. The growth tapered off to about 45 millimeters at the edges of the tray. In the control tray, growth was about 45 millimeters.

Objections arise as to this experiment, however. For instance, there was no control that would rule out the effects discovered by researchers Franklin Loehr and Cleve Backster —if, indeed, they are not the same. Loehr discovered the "power-of-prayer-on-plants" and Backster measured the response of plants to human sentiment by electronic instrumentation. It is not improbable that hope and expectations, even at an unconscious level, played some part in the difference in germination times. There is also the chance that trace elements having a beneficial effect on plants might have been present in the charged rod and not in the other. A new approach was planned.

This involved charging a pint of water in a pyramid and leaving another pint in a control box for three weeks. Both containers were stoppered. Sixteen two-ounce plastic vials were obtained from a pharmacy. They had broad white plastic caps. A similar number of well-circulated one-dollar bills were obtained from a bank. The last three serial digits of each were copied on to each of the vial caps, providing a quasi-random numbering system for later identification. In my absence, an assistant filled eight of the vials from the pyramid water and eight from the control water. Picking caps at random from within a paper bag, she sealed all of the vials, recording the numbers of those containing the pyramid water, and sealing the record in a double envelope. This had the effect of presenting me with a coded system in which no set of digits could be linked to any other and thus eliminated the chance of sentiment activating the Loehr or Backster effects.

Soaked and drained sunflower seeds were placed between layers of blotting paper and each identified with a set of digits from a given vial. The corresponding vial was used to water the seed. Small quantities of water were added as each paper became dry. It soon became clear that half of the sixteen seed packets were germinating more quickly than the others. At this point the experiment was terminated due to the possibility of unconsciously "cheering on" those seeds which germinated first. *In every case of early germination the seed was identified as having been watered from the pyramid-charged supply.*

As this seemed to indicate that water treated in a pyramid form is somehow altered, the question of *How?* arises. It would seem from experiments on meat that water tends to evaporate faster in a pyramid, thus producing the characteristic desiccation and shrinkage. A 100-milliliter graduate of water was placed in a pyramid form; another was placed in a box form of similar height at the same time. The graduate in the box lost 12 milliliters overnight; that in the pyramid lost 17.

This would seem to indicate a reduction of surface tension in the water, in turn implying a reduction in molecular cohesion. A fair test seemed to be to drop samples of both pyramid and control water onto oiled surfaces to see if there was a difference in droplet form. Distilled water obtained from a pharmacy was treated in stoppered containers in both control box and pyramid for four weeks. At the end of that time plates of clean glass were immersed in the same bath of mink oil (which is extremely resistant, if not actually impervious to oxidation) obtained from a pharmaceutical supplier. Both plates were suspended by 35-millimeter photographic clips to drain. Capillary pipettes were used to drop samples of each water onto the drained plates. The droplets of pyramid water were flatter and broader by 50 percent than those of the control water. This seems to me to be consonant with the view that a system which absorbs energy tends to expand and that the H-OH bond may be loosened to some degree in the pyramid water.

An interesting study, and one which has yet to be undertaken by me, would be to see how long the pyramid water droplets continued to flatten after the water was removed from treatment. Some evidence has been adduced by independent researchers which tends to support the claim that pyramid water has curative value when applied to cuts and bruises. If so, it would seem that a stored energy is released.

I swabbed an area on my left forearm with isobutyl alcohol and made two one-inch cuts—really no more than deep scratches—with the triangular blade of an Xacto knife. Bleeding was capillary and minimal. I swabbed one cut with surgical cotton that had been soaked in pyramid water and the other with cotton soaked in distilled control water. I covered each with a compress of surgical gauze, the one dampened with pyramid water and the other dampened with the control water. I retired for the night.

In the morning, the cut that had been treated with pyramid water seemed to be healing quite well with no sign of a crusted scab. The other was marked by a thin encrustation of scab and itched slightly. In twenty-four hours, the first cut was barely perceptible; the second had lost its encrustation but was still marked by a fine pink line that remained visible for another thirty-six hours.

It is easy to conceive of such an experiment as being dramatic, but it is hardly conclusive. Autosuggestion may have

been at work in a manner analogous to that by which some
dentists staunch the flow of blood by hypnosis.

I had no luck at all in any dowsing experiments, either in
the vicinity of the pyramids themselves or in those of variou
metal pieces that had been treated in them for some time
Nor did I notice that a magnetized steel needle gave any sig
of paying attention to them. However, I have never had
any success in dowsing for anything, anyway. Many experi
menters report using dowsing techniques to map out the
varying areas of power within pyramids and claim consider
able success.

There being suggestive evidence that some form of energy
transfer took place in the pyramid form, it occurred to me to
see if it would register photographically. Under darkroom
illumination I suspended strips of photographic enlarging pa
per from the apex of the pyramid and from the top of
rectangular control box. Forty-eight hours later, I develope
each strip. Surprisingly, the pyramid strip developed to
sparkling white, showing its halide grains were unaffected b
the energy within the structure. The control strip bore a fain
fogging in the form of swirling clouds. Investigation reveale
that the control box had been used previously for a mea
experiment, however, and I suspect amines from the decayin
protein may have permeated the bristol board and catalyze
the paper emulsion. A rerun with a new control box resulte
in no fogging.

By making tall-stemmed T-cuts, with the crossbar at th
King's Chamber level, I was able to insert an unspooled loo
of recording tape from a cassette. I let the tape remain mo
tionless for two days, but no spot of extraneous noise ap
peared upon replay.

Using a 1 N 64 Germanium diode input placed at chambe
level and feeding it into a tape recorder (after the manne
of some Raudive experiments) brought me no revelation
from a pharaonic Otherworld.

A charged electrolytic capacitor discharged at the sam
rate within the pyramid as it did when outside.

These experiments suggested to me that whatever energ
is at work within the pyramidal form, it cannot be classifie
as electromagnetic.

With but little confidence in the outcome, I tried sleepin
with my head inside a pyramid form on two successive night
On both occasions, though, I was rewarded with particular
vivid dream sequences. The dreams were remarkable in tha

they did not contain any of the fantasy quality that dreams usually offer. That is, upon awakening, every element of them could be recalled exactly as if it represented some prosaic bit of normal waking life. Unusually, both dreams were in vivid, though realistic color.

I was unable to make any reliable determination as to whether fluids stored in the pyramid undergo a change in taste. Any perceptible change could have been due to one of two factors. Aeration of the liquid surface might cause a change as it does when a dinner wine is opened a half hour before serving. In the case of water, exhalation of chlorine and aeration of other impurities might account for the taste. Though I noticed a definite change in taste in wine and water, it was not possible to distinguish between pyramid and control samples.

Pyramid water frozen into ice cubes resulted in a clearer product than those frozen from tap water. I attribute that to the loss of gases and not to pyramid energy. Placing three such cubes in a squat tumbler, I inundated them with three fluid ounces of Dewar's White Label, a spirituous liquor. The presence of the cubes made no perceptible difference in taste. Repeating the experiment, I relaxed and began to inquire of myself the implications of energy manifestations within the pyramidal form.

It seems useful at this point to examine some recondite but compelling evidence regarding the Great Pyramid; this with the idea that it may aid in defining a field in which the peculiar energy may be more easily understood.

Herodotus has told us that the Great Pyramid was built in twenty years. If so, it was a remarkable accomplishment. The structure contains 2.6 million blocks of stone, and there are only 10.5 million minutes in twenty years. *This suggests that the blocks were quarried, dressed, transported, hoisted, and placed at the rate of one every four minutes—allowing a work force that labored round-the-clock, day and night, for two decades.*

Egyptian records put down Cheops or Khufu, the pharaoh said to have built the pyramid, as having reigned for twenty-three years—2900 to 2877 B.C. So, even if he began the thing the moment he was crowned, his twenty-four-hour work force would have had to place those blocks at the rate of one every four minutes forty seconds in order to have it ready by the moment he died.

Since a feat of that order is manifestly impossible, it i
clear that Cheops did not build the Great Pyramid.

The only evidence that Cheops had anything to do with th
Great Pyramid is the fact that his name was found painte
on one of its passage walls. That is no evidence at all, fo
as Professor J. H. Breasted pointed out in his treatment c
the *Pyramid Texts* in his *Development of Religion an
Thought in Ancient Egypt,* even latter-day Egyptians believe
they visited Cheops's tomb because they found his name i
it. Actually, it was the tomb of a Seventeenth Dynasty nobl
man. So the presence of the Cheops cartouche, in itself, i
meaningless.

A faint glimmer of light blooms in an antique papyrus av
thored by one Hardefef, a son of Cheops. He cited a very ol
writing that had been found in *"the apex (benben) of th
mountain (ben) uncovered by my father."* Breasted (o
cit.) authenticates the story. The word *ben* or "mountain
was quite commonly used to designate "pyramid" by th
ancient Egyptians.

This suggests that Cheops did not build the Great Pyrami
but uncovered it. And it may be noted that, even in Dynasti
times, both pyramid and Sphinx occasionally were buried o
of sight by drifting desert sands. Anyway, Cheops had
name for refurbishing temples and other structures in an
around Gizeh. There are Egyptian records of that. There
no record of his having built a pyramid.

Then *who* built it?

I am no gods-from-space buff. In fact, I reject that enti
schmier out of hand on the basis of Occam's Law, but I d
believe there is a cogent body of evidence that suggests th
existence of a well-developed civilization before our ow
Other writers have gone into this extensively, and I have n
space to do so here. But it is my idea that about 10,00
B.C. our moon came tooling in from outer space, got bange
up in passing through the asteroid belt, and was picked v
by our gravitational field. I was tickled to find out that Profe
sor Harold Urey, a Nobel Prize-winner at the Universi
of Chicago, goes along with this.

The effect of the moon-capture would have been, first,
cause a crust slippage here on earth, and then, to pile up a
the waters and atmosphere and drag them round and rour
our globe in a relatively narrow belt. See the authoriti
cited by Ignatius Donnelly, Immanuel Velikovsky, and other

About the only things that could have been expected

Great Pyramid of Egypt, with Sphinx.

Contemporary view of the Pyramid of Kephren, with limestone casing on top. PHOTO: BARBARA BRIER

The main pyramid sites of the Old and Middle Kingdoms of Egypt.

Czecholoslovak radio engineer Karel Drbal, seated at his desk in the study where he perfected the design and theoretical description of a pyramid capable of keeping razor blades sharpened significantly beyond their standard period of optimum function. To the right is one of the Drbal pyramids. PHOTO: MLADY SVET

The age-old pyramid symbol has been incorporated into the design of the reverse side of the Great Seal of the United States. It can be found on official documents, as well as printed on paper currency, such as the left panel of the reverse of the one-dollar bill. The Latin words "Annuit Coeptis" stand for "He has blessed our efforts," while "Novus Ordo Seclorum" means "Age of New Order." The Roman numerals at the bottom of the pyramid, MDCCLXXVI, represent 1776, the U.S. Year of Independence.

Serge King, who describes a variety of pyramid experiments in this volume, is shown here examining a Kennedy half-dollar that had been placed inside a pyramid in a tarnished state. The coin regained its brilliance, which was exposed when King simply rubbed his thumb once across the coin. The coin is placed on a styrofoam block, one third up from the base line of the pyramid. PHOTO: ED IKUTA

Eric McLuhan, Canadian researcher, is shown with one of his experimental pyramids in an outdoor setting near his home in London, Ontario. PHOTO COURTESY En Route MAGAZINE

G. Patrick Flanagan, who expressed his evolving views on the impact of various physical shapes in the books Pyramid Power and Beyond Pyramid Power, states that his experiments have convinced him of "the relationship of biocosmic energy to the energy forces in living organisms." He directs Source of Innergy, Inc., in Los Angeles, California.

Sheila Ostrander, who, together with Lynn Schroeder (right), interviewed eastern European pyramid researchers and made their efforts known to an English-speaking public.

Lynn Schroeder, co-author of Psychic Discoveries Behind the Iron Curtain, *which was instrumental in creating interest in Czechoslovak pyramid studies among scientists and laymen in western Europe and the United States.* PHOTO: HOAG LEWIS

Dr. A. R. G. Owen (right), professor of mathematics at the University of Toronto, together with his wife, Iris Owen, whose report in this volume deals with the pyramid experiments undertaken by the New Horizon's Foundation of Toronto, Ontario (Canada). Ms. Owen holds one of the pyramids used in a series of tests. D & T FREELANCE PHOTOGRAPHY

Martin Gardner, columnist of Scientific American, *severe critic of pyramidology and historian of scientific fads and fallacies.*
PHOTO: BRAMSON STUDIOS

Max Toth, the New Yorker whose personal odyssey into the study of pyramidology led him into the construction and distribution of miniature pyramids in the United States.

survive a cataclysm like that would be the Great Pyramid and the platform at Baalbek. Macchu Pichu and Tiahuanaco were shoved two miles in the air by the rising Andes, too; but that's beside our point. A gang of mammoths were flash-frozen in northern Siberia when the protective atmosphere was yanked away, exposing them to the absolute zero cold of outer space. You can forget them, too. The idea is simply that all hell broke loose before the moon found its point of equilibrium 186 thousand miles away. Not many people survived. We lost the whole Cro-Magnon race, a people with a greater cranial capacity than our own.

Sir Flinders Petrie and Dr. Margaret Murray, a remarkable woman who was less than five feet tall and lived to be a hundred years old, adduced a lot of evidence that the people who settled in the Nile Delta originally came from the Caucasus. Other scholars point to demonstrable connections between Egypt and India, citing the antics of a Prince Nahusha after whom the Nile was said to have been named. One of the best bits of Caucasus evidence is the existence of a primeval Egyptian house god, Bes, who looked like no other Egyptian god at all but had definite Indo-Iranian characteristics. His statues—pop-eyes, bestial smirk, lolling tongue, and dangling phallus—have been found in the Caucasus area.

I think an allowable reconstruction is this: after the cataclysm, certain survivors in the Caucasus went down into Egypt land, an event tradition refers to as "when the gods went into Egypt." They settled in the Delta. Later, two different groups arrived from India entering Africa through (and probably founding) Saba or Sheba. One of these groups defeated the other and marched north under a general named Narmer or Menes. He wiped out the northern population or drove them from the land—some of the refugees probably founding Sumer. The viciousness of his onslaught is depicted in the slate known as "Narmer's palette," illustrations of which appear in practically every text on Egyptology.

Now the Great Pyramid may or may not have been built by the people of Egypt before the cataclysm. Evidence from its orientation has led many people to believe that it was. However, it may just as well have been built by those people who came down from the Caucasus and perhaps that view is preferable if we want to develop any coherent train of ancient knowledge. From 10,000 B.C. to Narmer's time is a period forty percent longer than that running from his time to our own: plenty of time to develop a sophisticated civilization and one quite capable of erecting the Gizeh structure.

Remarkably, though, that civilization's culture, though absorbed by the conquerors, seems never to have been fully understood by them. We know that because the dynastic civilization never developed. It appears on the historical horizon fully equipped with a language that had already begun to show decadent forms, with an architectural philosophy, with a literature and a poetry, with anesthesia, brain surgery, and a cure for cancer that was still in widespread use in our own world a century ago.

But the dynastic civilization never went anywhere. It never improved anything it had. It was as if it had inherited a body of knowledge beyond its comprehension, a way of doing things without understanding their rationale. It became a crime, a sacrilege, even, to try to change anything at all.

What little remained of the roots of dynastic culture was in the custody of the priesthood and remained secret. However, after the Persian invasions, when Egypt began to fall apart, those secrets began to leak out. The first one to carry away a bundle of them was Pythagoras. Many other Greek philosophers aped him, including Plato and Aristotle. The result of this was the formation of many schools of thought, each of which contained at least some shards of the fractured body of primevel learning. Much of this passed into the various Gnostic, Cabalistic, and Hermetic academies of the great cultural center at Alexandria. Later it was to be picked up by invading Moslems. Finally, it began to find its way into late Medieval and Renaissance Europe.

Now it may seem that I have led you far afield from the piece of meat that did not give me botulism, but my purpose has been to clear the way for the development of an energy concept that, it seems to me, may have a great deal to do with "pyramid power."

Renaissance teaching wrapped up these notes from ancient lore. The cosmos is a unity of *prime matter*. That matter is given its various identities by a principle called *form*. In its densest manifestation, the cosmic material is called, simply, *matter*. Its most tenuous manifestation is called *spirit*. Form, as a purely abstract principle, was pure spirit and, in some schools, was called God. Salvation lay in shaking off the material element of the cosmic unity and reuniting with the pure form element.

Now the concept of energy was but vaguely understood

by the ancients and by the Renaissance thinkers. About all that they knew was that if they poked something hard enough to overcome its inertia, the thing would move. They knew of action-at-a-distance only in terms of the lodestone's magnetism.

In the sixteenth century, Abbot Johann Trithemius, Bishop Cornelius Agrippa, and the devil-dealing Dr. Johann Faust, a trio who had probed deeply in the darker corners of natural philosophy, trained a young man who adopted the name of Paracelsus. By this time, the art of printing had hit its stride, and so the ideas of Paracelsus gained currency through books instead of through manuscripts restricted to a very small circle of readers.

Paramount among Paracelsian teachings was the idea of a tenuous substance occupying all space and permeating all matter. Through this substance a mysterious energy was believed to work.

A student of Paracelsus's philosophy, a Netherlander named Jan Battista van Helmont, explored the concept further, linking it to living tissue. Since the only force known that could achieve action-at-a-distance was magnetism, van Helmont called the unknown *animal magnetism*. He said, "It is active everywhere and has nothing new but the name; it is a paradox only to those who ridicule everything and attribute to Satan whatever they themselves are unable to explain."

Not until a century later was this concept picked up again, this time by the Viennese physician Franz Anton Mesmer. It was his idea that the peculiar energy could be used in therapy and the famous system of mesmerism or "magnetic healing" resulted.

But, from his studies of the energy involved, Mesmer learned certain things about it. For one thing, it permeates the entire cosmos. It is real enough to be reflected by mirrors and this implies that it can be focused by a lens system. It can be used to cure or kill. It can be stored in stone, metal, and plant and animal fibers and can be conducted by these. Now note this particularly: *it accompanies light and magnetism but is a complete and different type of energy and can operate independently of them.*

I do not intend here to go into the experiments of Reichenbach, who called the energy "Od," or of Reich, who called it "Orgone": these are treated extensively elsewhere. But it seems clear that they worked with the same energy. Instead, I prefer to develop the thesis that it is this energy that is active within the pyramid form and that it is the function of the pyramid form itself to provide a focal point of electromagnetic energy that carries with it, as if it were a conductor, a quantity of the peculiar pyramid energy.

In a book intended for a lay readership, I must, in this essay, gloss over the mathematical development of this thesis and depend upon correspondences and analogies.

First of all, consider that the pyramid energy (PE) *accompanies* electromagnetic energy, as noted above. It is said that it differs from electromagnetic energy, but I am inclined to question this. It is my belief that electromagnetic energy and PE represent only different dimensions along which a universal energy can manifest. Let me try to clarify that.

Grant me a miniature battery of, say, 1.5 volts and with enough electricity in it to give a current of only 150 milliamperes. If I touch the probes of an ordinary multimeter to the battery's terminals, while the meter is set on the voltage scale, I will get a reading of 1.5 volts, the *strength* of the current. When I turn the meter knob to the milliampere scale, I get a reading of 150 milliamperes, or the rate of *current flow*. These are two entirely different things.

Now the field of electric energy is the same and works through the innards of the meter on the same principle of the same d'Arsonval movement within it. The only true difference lies in the dimension along which the battery's electrical field is measured.

By feeding the battery's electricity into an oscillator and from thence into a high-frequency coil of the Tesla type, I can alter the relative dimensional measurements of the original field. (I ask professionals to bear with this oversimplification while I make a point.) I can, for example, step the strength of the current up to 150 thousand volts while at the same time reducing the current to 1½ millionths of an ampere. The electrical field is the same in its totality, only its dimensions have been altered.

The strength of the new field has certain applications of which the original field was incapable; for instance, it can be used to take Kirlian photographs. The current, however, has been reduced to a dimension which only relatively sophisticated instrumentation can detect.

I feel that something of this sort takes place within the pyramid form; that is, a relatively meager electromagnetic field is made to carry a proportionately much larger PE field.

Now that is all very well, of course; the question is, where does the electromagnetic field come from?

From quantum field theory we know that every particle of matter generates its own electromagnetic field, with millions of millions of cycles per second (nanoherz). Anything shaped in the form of a pyramid of the Gizeh proportions will have a focal point of maximum field strength on the apex-base axis of the pyramid and at the equivalent King's Chamber level.

Now, in the Gizeh Pyramid we have a situation where we have a concentration of electromagnetic energy at King's Chamber level. Measured along another dimension, that energy can be expressed as PE. As in our battery example, the electromagnetic component can be meager and the PE enormous. But how could this step-up be achieved?

I'll ask you to look at the illustration accompanying this essay and observe something that I do not believe any previous writer has commented upon, that is, the disposition of the various chambers within the pyramid itself. Observe the position of the King's Chamber and of the spaces above it. Notice that those spaces are separated by slabs of rock. It has been speculated that those spaces served to lighten the weight of the rock above the King's Chamber. I would have accepted that except for their cross section. To me, they look like *lenses*. The gabled structure above them looks like a reflection surface.

Now if we assume the chamber cut below the level of the pyramid base to be a kind of resonance chamber, we can start looking at the entire pyramid as a kind of energy transducing and concentrating device. Here is how it would work.

Energy focused at the King's Chamber would tend to diffuse in all directions, but mostly along the line of least resistance—i.e., vertically through the superior chambers. Here it would diffuse, due to the plano-convex shape of the intervening rock floors, but would still proceed upward until it met the gabled reflectors and two hundred feet of solid rock above them. As energy was reflected downward, the lenses would focus it in parallel beams, passing through the King's Chamber and downward through the pyramid base to the small underground chamber below.

The small chamber would serve as a resonator; that is, it would tend to reinforce the waves of energy entering it and

send them upward again. The entire process would be repeated, the result being a column of intense PE passing
through the King's Chamber.

If it be objected that the pyramid apex, King's Chamber,
and "pit" are not on an exact vertical, I would like to note
that it is possible to draw a series of reflected lines which pass
through all, though this results in a diagram too complicated
for practical presentation here.

Let us turn now to the possible uses which the Great
Pyramid might have served. I do not believe that the pre-
Dynastic Egyptians or even pre-cataclysmic Egyptians used
the Great Pyramid either to preserve hamburger or to sharp-
en razor blades. I do not believe that either pharaoh or high
priest lay in the King's Chamber sarcophagus to meditate.
The column of energy, continually reinforcing itself, would
have been too intense.

There is always the chance that the PE column might
have been used for the transmutation of metals, but even this
would not have justified the expense of the enormous structure.

It seems most likely that the Great Pyramid served as a
power plant for charging various storage devices that could
be placed in the King's Chamber sarcophagus. The storage
devices could then be removed and used for whatever purpose they were planned—the preservation of food, therapeutic treatments, or, given the proper transducing equipment,
motive power.

Here we reach a limit as far as the possible application of
pyramid power is concerned. The devices we construct of
plastic or cardboard can give only the meagerest hints as
to what the power could do at maximum intensity. Until we
start building scale models of the Gizeh Pyramid using the
same limestone and granite of which it is built, we can only
speculate.

In our speculations, though, we ought not to overlook
possible consciousness-altering effects of the PE, though it
seems to me remote indeed that the original structure was
intended as a mammoth psychedelic device. Still, anecdotal
literature is full of tales involving extraordinary effects on
the minds of those who stayed in the pyramid for any length
of time. These, it seems to me, must have been side effects
but, nonetheless, side effects worthy of explanation.

Of the anecdotes there are many with an obviously high
garbage coefficient; but there are others that seem worthy of

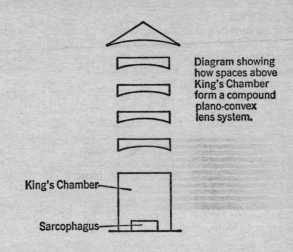

Diagram showing how spaces above King's Chamber form a compound plano-convex lens system.

King's Chamber

Sarcophagus

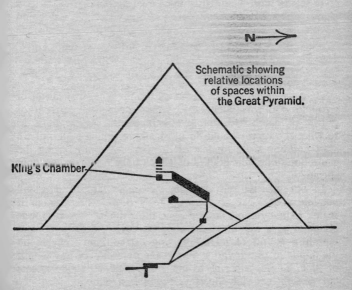

N →

Schematic showing relative locations of spaces within the Great Pyramid.

King's Chamber

study. In the 1830's a sea captain, G. B. Caviglia, lived in the Great Pyramid for a time and had experiences that left him shaken, but which he would never discuss. Aleister Crowley and his bride, Rose Kelly, spent a night in the King's Chamber. She developed unexpected mediumistic powers and produced the eldritch *Book of the Law* at the reputed dictation of an entity known as Aiwass.

But, perhaps the most eerie events of all involved the hardheaded Napoleon Bonaparte. In 1798, on his Egyptian expedition, Napoleon asked his aides to leave him so that he might spend some time alone in the pyramid. When, at length, he emerged, he was quite visibly upset, pallid and withdrawn. Asked if he had had any unusual experience, he retorted sharply that he had no comment to make and did not want the matter brought up again.

Though he never detailed his experience, Napoleon let slip hints that he had seen something of his future in the Great Pyramid. While he was exiled on St. Helena, dictating some of his memoirs to the French historian Comte de La Cases, he seemed to be on the verge of revealing his experience. Then he shrugged and said, "But to what avail? No, you'd never believe me . . ."

From the experiments I conducted with the pyramid form, and in view of the evidences coming down through the ages as to an extraordinary manifestation of energy, it seems to me that such a thing as is popularly called "pyramid power" actually exists. This is not to be construed as an endorsement of the claims that have been advanced by a multitude of mystical featherheads, but is intended to be a conservative assessment of an inescapable reality: a form of energy field outside of the electromagnetic exists within a pyramidal form.

As to whether or not that energy can be harnessed depends upon how well we come to understand its nature. Here a need for extensive and rigidly controlled experimentation is indicated.

My Research Odyssey

by Max Toth

How did one of the world's leading pyramid researchers happen to become interested in this suddenly so popular subject? Mr. Toth, president of the Toth Pyramid Company of Bellerose, N.Y., describes how his early fascination with parapsychology and various arcane areas of study propelled him into firsthand contact with the Czechoslovak patent holder of power pyramids. Together with Greg Nielson, the author has written a book, Pyramid Power, *published by Inner Traditions International, 377 Park Avenue South, New York, N.Y. 10016. Mr. Toth has been instrumental in arranging the first and second International Congress on Psychotronic Research; the meetings have been notable as a forum for researchers from eastern European countries as well as from western Europe and the United States.*

I have had an interest in parapsychology (now sometimes called "psychotronics") since my teens, but I did not realize the significance of the events responsible for my odyssey into pyramid research, psychotronics, and the psychic world until after it was firmly established. I was initially fascinated by the works of Frank Edwards, John Keel, and Charles Fort, which dealt with mysterious occurrences throughout the world, particularly vanishing ships and planes.

After earning an associate degree in electronics, I worked in medical electronics although I planned to become either an accountant or a lawyer. Instead, I joined the Air National Guard and served as an airborne radio radar technician for two and a half years. After this, I again became involved in medical electronics, working with neurosurgical teams that researched the cause and alleviation of epilepsy. With my knowledge of brain waves, or electroencephalograms (EEG), it was an easy step into sleep research: a physician and his associate invited me to collaborate in research at City College, New York, studying psychological effects of dream deprivation.

While monitoring reports of the dreams (called "mentations") of the awakened subject, so many of the reports were incredibly realistic and natural that I began to wonder whether these events could actually have taken place, perhaps as an out-of-body experience on some other plane. My query was enhanced when I met Dr. Stanley Krippner of the Maimonides Dream Laboratory, and learned of his ESP experiments during a subject's dream state. As the subject dreamed, a sender in another room attempted to send telepathically a visualized image of a target picture (for example, a photo, postcard, or artwork). The results of these experiments were statistically significant.

While pursuing my graduate studies in experimental psychology at New York University, I joined the American Society for Psychical Research. There I met a researcher who was conducting ESP and clairvoyance experiments and out-of-body experiences and who was using the polygraph, the same instrument used to record brain waves. I then decided to donate my services to this organization to learn more about these unusual phenomena.

I also began avidly reading in the Eileen J. Garrett Memorial Library, and elsewhere, on all facets of parapsychology. My fascination with pyramids and pyramid energy slowly increased with each book I read on the subject. However, my curiosity and frustration grew as the number of unanswered questions overwhelmed me. Who built the pyramids, and how? Why so many? What purpose did they serve? These were only a few of the questions I pondered, but the one that sparked my interest most was: What were the sources of the strange energies and powers of the pyramids that could perfectly mummify human bodies, dehydrate foods and grains which showed no decay thousands of years later? There was even a report of a Czechoslovakian patent on a pyramid-shaped razor blade sharpener. Now, this was something I could readily relate to: energies manifested within the pyramid, or emanating from the top or around the pyramid-shaped model, just a four-sided, sloped structure built to the scale of the Cheops Pyramid. Here, indeed, was something tangible that I could work with on my own, using my technical knowledge to experiment and see for myself what these energies were capable of and to what degree.

Barely a year later, in the summer of 1971, my semi-invalid father asked me to accompany him to Budapest, his native city, to visit relatives whom he had not seen in thirty-five years. This would enable me to visit some of the Czech pyramid researchers. An associate of mine kindly provided me with the address and phone number of Dr. Zdeněk Rejdák. I knew Dr. Rejdák to be one of the best-informed persons on parapsychology in all of eastern Europe, and he might introduce me to Dr. Karel Drbal, inventor of the pyramid razor blade sharpener.

I arrived in Budapest with my father and settled him comfortably with our relatives. After obtaining a visa for Czechoslovakia, I set out on the trip which later would prove to be one of the most fruitful ventures in my odyssey into pyramid research. Locomotive difficulties stretched the eight-hour train ride to twenty-four hours, so that I found myself in Prague at six o'clock in the morning. There are not many people around at this hour who speak English. Using my high school German, I was able to ask directions and find the way to my hotel.

The next morning, I awakened eager to meet Dr. Rejdák. The hotel clerk telephoned his house for me, and Mrs. Rejdák informed us that her husband would be at work all day. She suggested that I stop by around five in the evening. So I spent the day in the usual tourist fashion, visiting the museum, the famous clock at the center of old town and the ancient Karlštejn Castle, until it was time to take a taxi to meet Zdeněk Rejdák. My excitement mounted as I enjoyed the ride through the picturesque countryside of the tiny suburb on the outskirts of Prague. His house is tucked away on a charming street leading off a winding road.

Dr. Rejdák arrived just a few minutes after I did. He is a fairly tall man in his mid-thirties, with blond hair, sparkling blue eyes, and a friendly smile. At first, we had a communication problem, but after an hour or so, we found ourselves tuning in to each other. With our mutual high-school level German, his several words of English, some Hungarian, and the help of a Czech-English dictionary, our exchange of information managed to flow along.

I was impressed with the scope and wealth of knowledge Zdeněk possessed and willingly shared with me. First, we discussed the work of Valentina and Semyon Kirlian in the USSR, who had photographed energy emanating from a leaf, a human finger, or an inanimate object, for example, a coin. Some call this energy the aura, bioplasmic energy, or corona discharge. Next, Rejdák briefly mentioned the psychotronic generators discovered by Dr. Robert Pavlita in Czechoslovakia. These metallic devices are able to store energy and release it for some specific function, such as operating relays or solenoids by remote control, at a later time. We also discussed experiments paralleling those of Cleve Backster and Marcel Vogel in the United States, dealing with cell and plant communication, commonly called "emotions of plants." Then, Zdeněk described the strange ability of Madame Nelya Mikhalova (Nina Kulagina) of Leningrad, to move objects without touching them. After this, the subject turned to pyramid energy. We talked into the early morning hours and probably would have talked the night through, except that Zdeněk had to work the following day. He drove me back to my hotel, but before saying good night, he invited me for lunch, to which he promised to bring an interesting guest he was sure I would be pleased to meet.

And pleased I was, when at lunch he introduced me to Engineer Karel Drbal, who is considered to be the "father of radio engineering" in Czechoslovakia, but who was most important to me because he is the patent holder of the razor blade sharpener. Engineer Drbal explained that it had taken ten years for the Czech patent to finally be approved and issued. Approval was based on the ability of the structure (a model of the Cheops Pyramid, made to scale), or the energy within the structure, to sharpen dull razor blades. But beyond this, Drbal had discovered he could dehydrate or mummify flowers and other specimens, using a face angle of no less than twenty-five degrees and no more than seventy-five. He also proved that atmospheric changes affect the functioning properties of the pyramid model as well as cosmic variations of planetary positions and the positions of comets and meteors to earth.

During the next few days, I met as often as possible with Karel and Zdeněk. Drbal showed me the now legendary razor blade he had used for at least 250 shaves. He also displayed many of the specimens he had dehydrated, using his pyramid models. During our conversation, Karel confirmed my hypothesis that different energies existed in different-shaped structures. He postulated that square rooms may not really provide optimum environment; circular structures might be better, because they are psychologically more appealing.

In turn, I shared my learning experiences in physiological recording techniques and my theories relating to the electrical activity of the body with electrostatic voltages and magnetic energies. I explained that I felt the energies involved in psychic healing, psychokinesis (PK), Kirlian photographic images, and psychotronic generators are all tied to the basic ability of a person to alter the electrical activity throughout his body. Both Zdeněk and Karel agreed.

On the last evening of my stay, my hosts announced they would like to entrust me with the U.S. rights to Drbal's Czech patent of the pyramid model. They asked me if I would be willing to investigate the possibilities of manufacturing and marketing the pyramid model, since they were no longer available in Czechoslovakia. I was surprised but pleased and honored by their offer. Still, I wondered why they had selected me for this project. They felt that with my technical knowledge of electronics, my growing psychotronic background, and my ability to communicate with them, I would be able to carry out valuable research, perhaps work out some of my own hypotheses, and also bring information about pyramid energy to large numbers of people in the West. I enthusiastically accepted their generous offer and promised to let them know the results of my investigation as soon as possible.

If I had not had to pick up my father who was ready to return to the United States, I would have extended my visit in Prague. Promising to return, I reluctantly left for Budapest. On the way, however, I stopped in Bratislava to meet Dr. Julius Krmessky, a mathematician and physicist who has been conducting research on energy radiating from human eyes. Simply stated, this energy is related to an experience you have probably had at some time or other while riding in a crowded subway train or bus: you suddenly sense that another person is staring at you and when your eyes search out that person, and locate him or her, the person turns away. This is often called the "Krmessky effect," or the "eyeball effect."

In the fall of 1971, I tried to duplicate the styrene model of the pyramid razor blade sharpener which I had brought back from Czechoslovakia. But the machine setup and die molds proved to be very costly. So, instead, I decided to design a less expensive and more practical cardboard model.

Cardboard, I discovered, is just as functional and perhaps more practical because it is easily assembled and folds neatly into an envelope for mailing. As long as the model is built to the exact scale of the Cheops Pyramid, it has the same properties and energy emissions, both inside and outside, as those of the original styrene model. Subsequently, I formed the Toth Pyramid Company in New York City and began manufacturing and marketing cardboard pyramid models. Since the end of 1971, Toth Pyramid models have been available in many bookstores, from other distributors, and by direct mail order.

As promised, the following spring I returned to Prague to personally report on the progress of the Toth Pyramid Company and to share the results of my research projects with Karel and Zdeněk. In addition, I had the opportunity of exchanging information with Dr. Krmessky and other scientists who were visiting Zdeněk at this time. They gave me suggestions for refining the Kirlian photographic device I had constructed and with which I had taken the very first Kirlian photo in New York City.

Of all the experiments I have done with the pyramid model, my favorite one is dehydrating or mummifying both fresh and salt water tropical fish. They become rock-hard, and although there is slight shrinkage and loss of color, they are otherwise perfectly preserved. During our discussions, I emphasized that, in order to obtain perfectly mummified or dehydrated specimens (for example, herbs, flowers, strawberries, mushrooms, and tropical fish), it is not essential to use the critical height of one third the distance from the base of the pyramid model. These specimens may simply be placed on the floor or base of the pyramid model, but one must take great care to align the model precisely with the cardinal points. For sharpening razor blades, however, it *is* essential to use the critical height of one third the distance from the base of the pyramid model.

In an interesting experiment I was able to demonstrate the energy emanating from the top of a pyramid. By placing a pyramid model in one of four identical boxes, and then holding a dowsing rod over each box for a moment or two, I could immediately tell which box contained the pyramid by the energy force field that moved the dowsing rod.

One evening, we viewed films of the renowned Russian PK expert, Madame Kulagina, performing psychokinesis under rigid scientific conditions and witnessed by Zdeněk. Krmessky then showed films of his research experiments on the eyeball energy phenomena. I reported that I had been able to demonstrate and duplicate his experiments successfully.

One of the highlights of the week was the day Zdeněk arranged a visit to the home of Dr. Robert Pavlita. I was thrilled to meet this fantastic inventor and his daughter Jana, who works closely with him, and to see firsthand the intricate functioning of his amazing and intriguing psychotronic generators. It was a rare privilege, indeed, to watch the demonstration of these beautifully executed devices that seemed to operate on pure psychic or stored human bioenergy.

As the week drew to a close, Zdeněk and I, both realizing the inestimable value of our exchange of information, simultaneously expressed the hope of setting up an international conference. We agreed it should be a working conference aimed at summarizing and evaluating the research results achieved thus far in this field, as well as determining future research trends. It would certainly be an exciting milestone in international scientific progress and cooperation. As secretary of the section for Psychotronic Research of the Committee on Applied Cybernetics of the Czech Society for Science and Technology, Zdeněk was in a favorable position to apply for government approval and support of our proposed conference.

I extended my visit for a few more days to give us time to work out the preliminary details of the various working sections: Physics, Man and Matter, Integral Anthropology and Medicine, ESP and Altered States of Consciousness, Radiesthesia and Dowsing, Pedagogy, and Interaction of Man and Nature. Participation and attendance would be by invitation. We prepared a list of eminent scientists and researchers whom we would invite to be section leaders, as well as a list of those we would invite to present scientific papers. The plans were made, and after many months of negotiating, they became a reality when the First International Conference on Psychotronic Research was held in Prague in June of 1973. Dr. Rejdák served as chairman of the Eastern Hemisphere and I, of course, served as chairman of the Western Hemisphere.

More than three hundred scientists and researchers arrived from twenty-two countries. One hundred and three research papers were presented. Indeed, we surpassed our highest expectations for hosting a successful exchange of experience and information in the true spirit of international cooperation and friendship. An International Association for Psychotronic Research was created to continue the exchange on a permanent basis, with a psychotronic research journal; a second conference was planned for 1975.

In my national lecture series during 1972 and 1973, I spoke on many subjects: psychotronic research, PK or telekinesis, Kirlian photography, psychotronic generators, and, of course, all the information I had gathered on pyramids and pyramid power. At these lectures, I met many persons who were experimenting with model pyramids and putting pyramid energy to functional use. They were dehydrating grapes, apples, mushrooms, herbs, and strawberries into condiments for cooking; mummifying flowers, energizing themselves, and using the large pyramid models to achieve greater levels of meditation, to mention just a few of the many interesting aspects. Research that had been conducted on an individual basis was subsequently verified as we exchanged results. We frequently exchanged data on experiments and discussed new ideas. I was always pleased to learn of someone's newest innovation.

When I renewed my acquaintance with an editor of *Esquire* magazine, he interviewed me about pyramids and pyramid energy and wrote a two-page article which appeared in the April, 1973, issue. It included a photograph of my clear plastic pyramid model, especially created to demonstrate that transparent material has the same properties as its nontransparent counterpart. This publicity led to numerous TV and radio interviews on both local and national stations.

In the summer of 1973, Greg Nielsen approached me with the idea of co-authoring a book on pyramid power. Even before the contract was signed, we were involved in enormous research for our book. Greg and I found interesting and contradicting information in the archaeological material on the pyramids as well as on the many various and curious uses of model pyramids. When our book *Pyramid Power* was reviewed in the summer of 1974, it was hailed as encyclopedic in content and set the pattern for the books that followed. It represented our efforts in gathering from around the world all the available information on pyramid research experiments —how to conduct them and how to use pyramid energy as well as the ancient legends and history of the pyramids, pyramid construction, pyramid patents, and pyramid models: in short, a source book for anyone interested in joining our adventure in pyramid discoveries.

Pyramid Power was the first such book to be distributed nationally and was an immediate success, selling out 100,-000 copies. Our research had come to fruition in this unexpected recognition of what was to me one of the most mysterious forces and greatest mysteries that the ancients left as a legacy for us. So keen is the interest in pyramid power today that Inner Traditions International has commissioned us to prepare a new, revised, and enlarged edition of our book. This will allow us to present the most current research and developments and to continue the narrative of our odyssey into Pyramidology. The odyssey will one day conclude with the realization of the dream that Karel, Greg, and I have long had: to visit the Pyramid of Gizeh to see, to explore, and to experience its strange energies firsthand, and then perhaps to visit all the other pyramids throughout the world.

Discussions in Moscow

by Benson Herbert

Mr. Herbert, director of the Paraphysical Laboratory, at Downton, Wiltshire (England), is active in an exchange of information between the countries of eastern and western Europe, as well as the United States. He edits the International Journal of Paraphysics, *which makes texts and summaries of material from the Soviet Union and other eastern nations available to an English-language audience. Benson Herbert attended a Moscow meeting from July 17 to 21, 1972, arranged by the Association for Humanistic Psychology, during which he reported on psycho-energetic studies and participated in discussions related to research in this field. His report on the Moscow talks concerning pyramid power illustrates a spirited give-and-take between researchers that is natural in such a controversial area of inquiry.*

One of the young scientists I met at the Moscow conference in 1972 was Engineer Jaroslav Mrkvicka, whom I had previously encountered at a cybernetics conference in Marienbad (Czechoslovakia) in October, 1971. At that meeting, the young Czech scientist had presented a paper on the practical uses of parapsychology, prepared in cooperation with Dr. Zdeněk Rejdák, one of Czechoslovakia's most prominent parapsychologists. In between, Mrkvicka had worked in Alma Ata, capital of the Soviet Republic of Kazakhstan, in Central Asia; now, we met again in Moscow. During our talks in Prague, I had become aware of his interest in the theories of Engineer Karel Drbal, an associate of Dr. Rejdák, on the alleged properties of pyramidal shapes. At the same time, I knew of the skepticism on this subject on the part of another

conference participant, Dr. Friedbert Karger, a nuclear physicist associated with the Max Planck Institute in Germany. I
therefore decided it would be fruitful to bring them together
for a discussion at a Moscow hotel.

Dr. Rejdák had shown me a document from the Czech
Patent Office, an official patent relating to Drbal's invention,
and had presented me with a sample pyramid made of red
plastic, hollow, standing on a white base 4½ inches square.
Each of the four sides of the pyramid consists of an equilater-
al triangle, length of one side $= 4¼$ inches. Inside the
pyramid, upon its base, stands a pedestal one inch high, upon
which the user lays a razor blade; it is claimed that if the long
side of the razor points to the north, the blade will remain
sharp indefinitely. It is claimed also that cheese, fish, etc., laid
on the pedestal will remain fresh for long periods.

This device, which we were to discuss, has achieved such
fame in the U.S.A. that the Toth Pyramid Company of New
York was formed to manufacture and sell cardboard replicas,
rather larger in size, the length of one side being 6 inches.
The director, Max Toth, was himself in Moscow for the
conference, and gives the following instructions to users of the
pyramid:

"Place the pyramid at least six feet from electrical apparatus and away from windows and radiators, and align the
blade to the magnetic north; mark one end of the blade for
north and maintain this orientation; leave the blade under the
pyramid for at least seven days before use. After a month of
use, the keenness will stabilize and will then remain consistent. For the preservation of flowers, eggs, meat, fish, etc.,
arrange that the longest axis of the specimen is centered on
the north-south line and that it does not extend beyond a
point 1¼ inches above the base. The dehydration process
averages 60 days depending upon the fluid weight of the
specimen. The dehydration processes are concentrated within
the lower third of the overall height of the pyramid."

Dr. Rejdák had stated that the notion began with observations made by a Monsieur Bovis who noticed that the
corpses of small animals in the Cheops Pyramid in Egypt
had become mummified, particularly in the pharaoh's chamber located at about one-third of the height of the pyramid
above the base. It is known that under certain conditions of
air currents, corpses may be preserved from decomposition,
but Drbal wondered if the actual shape and orientation of
the pyramid could influence the process.

On the European continent it is possible to obtain yoghurt in pyramidal containers. At the Paraphysical Laboratory we have carried out a number of rather inconclusive experiments with these pyramids, but this may be due to the damp atmosphere prevailing in the New Forest area, where our facilities are located.

Drbal even suggests that the conical shape of witches' hats may be beneficial and could cure headaches, though it is difficult to see how one could eliminate suggestion in this case. The general concept is that particular shapes may act as resonators of "psychotronic energy," and in Czechoslovakia they see here a connection with the experiments of Robert Pavlita. It is supposed that the ancient Egyptians were aware of this effect and designed their pyramids accordingly.

I confess that I remained skeptical, feeling that the experiments had not been performed under sufficiently controlled conditions, though when in Prague I was scarcely in a position to adopt a wholly negative attitude, for I realized that I myself had been airing not dissimilar ideas; in conversation with a young lady Yugoslav architect working in Prague, I had discussed the possibility of designing a Poltergeist House, of such a shape as to encourage paranormal incidents, a kind of scientific "House that Jack Built" incorporating architectural features that I had seen in certain "haunted" Scottish castles; I visualized these shapes as hypergeometrical sections.

I was, therefore, intrigued to see how Mrkvicka would fare under cross-examination from the skeptical Karger. I triggered the argument by mentioning that I had not so far been impressed by the pyramids. Mrkvicka replied with apparent conviction:

"I have carried out experiments with razor blades. The absolute dimensions of the pyramid are unimportant, the material is also unimportant. I used an opaque plastic material and chose kinds of fish which go bad very quickly, as well as razor blades. After one week the fish became completely dehydrated and did not go bad. For control, I used a similar piece of fish in the same room, lying half a meter away in a glass cylinder. I have a theory, not yet completely formulated, as an explanation for this effect. From the point of view of physics I would suggest it should be classed as paranormal. Just now I am working on the connection between information theory and geometry; under the pyramid we have a space with low entropy content, and under these conditions there could be a connection with bioenergetic processes."

Karger asked: "How is this information transferred to the object? It is not possible with electromagnetic waves."

Mrkvicka thought it was possible, and his theory considers the complex interaction of electromagnetic waves in a closed space. Karger continued: "If you assume then that it is an electromagnetic interaction, how do you make this interaction? You have a pyramid—what do you imagine is happening within it? The enclosure itself means nothing in this case."

Mrkvicka answered, "In thermodynamics, all events normally proceed with increasing entropy, but in living systems, one may reverse this process."

Karger then said, "I see no connection with the pyramid. If you wish to explain this in terms of known physics, you must relate the phenomena to the actual pyramid. Unless you say it is paranormal, like PK [psychokinesis] which we cannot explain by 'today's' physics, but perhaps by 'tomorrow's' physics. I am seeking ordinary physical interpretations, perhaps in one of the vessels there was more circulation of air. It would be necessary to make experiments with identical materials and to exclude air completely from both."

At this point I interrupted to say that the control in the glass vessel would be subject to heat and light radiation passing through the glass; it is known that ultraviolet components of light radiation will accelerate decomposition of organic matter; the only way to carry out the experiment properly is to use two vessels of the same opaque material, of identical thickness and volume, but of different forms, thus one could be pyramidal and the other cubic or spherical, etc. Only in this way could one discover whether the pyramidal shape makes any difference.

Karger agreed, adding: "In the case of a razor blade, recuperation can take place if the blade is left undisturbed in the air for a time; in three to four weeks, a blunted blade may become sharper by a spontaneous process; whiskers may grow from the edge of the blade; it is not an elastic deformation but a slow motion of the atoms of the metal, one sliding over another, in a restricted range. Under certain conditions there is a calculable probability that they will move and grow up to a certain point, then they can grow no more. If you examine the blade under the microscope, you may see fine needle-shapes sticking out. The razor is now sharper than before. Even a blade originally blunt can do this. It would be necessary to have two identical blades, one aligned north/south, the other east/west, to compare them and examine them microscopically. This would be better than merely trying to judge by shaving. Different people may have different shaving experiences."

On this, I commented: "In the model pyramid which I possess, the blade fits on to the platform in such a way that the cutting edges are not in contact with anything, the air has free play all round them; this is a different physical situation to that which usually applies, when the blade is left clamped into the razor, or left wrapped in paper, or otherwise not freely exposed to the air; perhaps under these conditions, the growth of microscopic needles is inhibited, and the blade will stay blunt."

Mrkvicka replied: "I would like to mention another experiment of Drbal's, in which he hung two similar pieces of meat on threads in the open air, 10 cm. apart. This was in an ordinary room with no curtains on the windows, so there was daylight alternating with darkness at night. But all the time, he had a ray of green light shining on one of the pieces, and the one with the green light on it stayed fresh, while the other decomposed. Other experiments have been carried out in Czechoslovakia on the quality of beer. Someone thought, why should beer always be kept in a round cask? So they tried altering the shape of the casks, but they found that when they used any other shape except the traditional one, the quality of the beer sank so low that it became undrinkable. This seems to show that the shape of a vessel may strongly influence its contents. Perhaps if beer were kept in pyramids, it would never mature at all, the same influence that keeps meat fresh may prevent the chemical processes in the beer from proceeding at their normal rate."

I said: "This is the first experiment on these lines which I have heard which really impresses me. I wonder if there is any connection between these ideas and orgone therapy. In Somerset, England, there is a man called Hugh Lodge who asks you to sit inside an orgone box; this is a cylinder three inches high and two inches wide, it consists of twelve alternate layers of wallpaper and tinfoil, covered on the outside with red fablon plastic. You sit on a chair and he puts the cylinder over your head so that the upper part of your body is right inside it. This is supposed to enhance ESP, and to facilitate diagnosis of disease, as well as having a therapeutic effect. Some people with minor complaints claimed to feel better inside it; I confess that when I sat inside it, all I felt was acute claustrophobia."

The orgone box has the wrong shape, we concluded. According to Drbal, an enclosure in spherical or pyramidal form would have a beneficial effect. Karger could not see how a plastic pyramid could resonate to electromagnetic waves. But if the psychokinetic phenomena of the Leningrad psychic Nina Kulagina involve some new kind of force-field, not electromagnetic in nature, and if this force-field can react to produce movements in nonmetallic and nonmagnetic objects, then it would be quite consistent with this hypothesis to suppose that "standing waves" of interference could be set up in vessels of certain shapes. For if the force-field can react with particles of matter, conversely matter such as the sides of a container could react with the field, causing reflection and refraction, and the production of resonances.

We concluded that many more carefully controlled experiments were needed to elucidate this possible connection between PK and Drbal's pyramid phenomena.

How Much Would It Cost to Build the Great Pyramid?

by Russ Martin

Let's assume the generation that put a man on the moon got it into its collective head to build a replica of the Great Pyramid of Cheops? Just how much would this project cost? Mr. Martin obtained estimates from experts in construction methods, labor costs, and architecture. Assuming the pyramid would most logically be placed in another desert, he chose Arizona as the most likely area; as this southwestern state's residents have shown considerable interest in pyramidology (see "Pyramids, Western Style," page 118), the authors' calculation has a nice touch of pseudo-realism. But even in this day of chronic inflation and governmental cost-overruns, the price of a U.S. pyramid turns out to be forbidding.

A mausoleum, as defined by Ambrose Bierce in *The Devil's Dictionary,* is "the final and funniest folly of the rich."

And the grandest mausoleum of them all is the Great Pyramid, built some 4,600 years ago by the Egyptian ruler Cheops, also known as Khufu, at the edge of the desert just outside Cairo's sister city of Gizeh.

Final? Certainly. The Great Pyramid was intended to be Cheops's funerary edifice, or so many claim, although it has not been established that the pharaoh's body ever rested within.

Funniest folly? It depends on one's point of view. Ambrose Bierce, after all, was a literary imp whose first choice of a title for his irreverent lexicon was *The Cynic's Word Book.*

Rich? Cheops had no worries on that score. His pyramid —some 480 feet high originally, and measuring 750 feet along the base—is so large it monopolized the labors of 100,000 workers for thirty years.

Pyramid-builders are a rare breed these days. But isn't it about time, in this age of technological achievement, that we build a *new* Great Pyramid?

A pyramid of our very own, right here in the United States?

Admittedly, the price tag would be high. But the task can be accomplished, and for that we have the word of Gordon H. Ball, Inc., of Danville, California, a Dillingham Corporation company whose expertise we engaged for our little architectural fantasy.

Where should we build it?

A geologist consulted by Gordon H. Ball suggests a site about seventeen miles southeast of Salome, Arizona, an area resembling the Egyptian desert from the standpoint of climate and geology. The land there has good drainage and the underlying rock doesn't tend to crack—problems that plagued the early Egyptians.

There are other advantages. This site is close to the route of Interstate 10, and not far from a railroad. In addition, travelers flying from Phoenix to Las Vegas will be able to look down and gaze upon it.

At $50 an acre—a value estimated by the Yuma County assessor—we'll need $64,000 worth, which measures out to two square miles.

Our next step is what construction people call "mobilization"—buying equipment, setting up camp, a power plant and workshop, extending trackage from Salome, and building and equipping a railroad yard.

This is all relatively inexpensive, and will set us back only $7,824,000, a sum that includes "demobilization," dismantling all the construction paraphernalia and cleaning up the site for the first onrush of tourists.

Before starting their colossus, Cheops's crew had to level their construction site to within a half-inch of true horizontal, and we must do the same. Not only is excavating necessary for a firm foundation, but it would be aesthetically *gauche* to have the finished pyramid sitting in a fifteen-foot hole. So the excavation must be graded over 135 acres, even though the pyramid base occupies only 13.1 acres.

This means, in short, that over three million cubic yards of sand must be pushed around. We have just spent another $6,469,000.

Fortunately, modern machinery is available for our twentieth-century project. We'll need twenty hoists, custom-designed for pyramid-building, to move 2½-to-3½-ton limestone blocks up the sides of the pyramid at a rate of 700 feet per minute. Once a stone has been lifted to the slab (the exposed level surface), we will move it into position with one of seventy rubber-tired, modified forklifts. Down below, another fifty forklifts will transfer stones from railroad cars to the base of the hoists. Between the forklifts and the hoists, it will be possible to place 2,400 or more stones daily.

The capstone or pyramidion—six and a half feet high and ten feet at the base—will be lowered into place by a construction-duty helicopter.

The entire modern-day operation, including maintaining and operating a railyard, and having engineering crews on hand to keep each layer of stones level, will require 405 men to do the work for which 100,000 ancient Egyptians were needed. But, of course, they didn't have forklifts.

Paying all these people and running the equipment will cost us about $55,411,000.

Now, about materials. Virtually all of the stone will be limestone, but instead of red granite on the apex, marble is recommended.

Just about any good construction-quality limestone will do for the interior stonework. For the facing, however, the best choice is statuary buff limestone, such as that used in the Empire State Building, the Pentagon, and the *Chicago Tribune* Tower.

The limestone will be expensive, because all dimensions must be cut within a 1/16th-of-an-inch tolerance. And the closest place to find ninety-one million cubic feet of good limestone is near Bedford, Indiana, at a cost of $6 per cubic foot. Four quarries will be needed, operating simultaneously in cutting the stone and stockpiling it so construction can continue during the winter when quarrying cannot. We will need nearly six million tons.

In transporting the stone from Indiana to Arizona, we can figure 1,500 stones in each trainload, and about four days to make the trip, at an estimated cost of $46.20 per ton.

Adding the cost of materials and shipping together, with an allowance for managing the entire process, we come up with a total of $897,872,000.

Gordon H. Ball suggests an allowance for escalation of labor expense, and a contingency sum to cover unforeseen increases in other expenses—an additional $15,295,000.

Based on a one-shift day (to avoid premium labor costs), and a construction year of 250 working days, it will take six years to build our pyramid. The first twelve months of that will be mobilization and preparation of the site, with another four months for moving out when the job is done.

The actual construction will take fifty-six months.

The people at Gordon H. Ball wisely point out that a project of this magnitude involves substantial risk, and the odd nature of this particular enterprise makes it even riskier. Hence, a suggested profit for the contractor of fifteen percent, or $147,455,000.

That puts our estimated expenditure at more than $1 billion. To be exact, a grand total of $1,130,390,000.

If that doesn't buy a Great Pyramid, at least it should buy a good one.

The Toronto Laboratory Tests

by Iris M. Owen

Mrs. Owen is secretary of the New Horizons Research Foundation of Toronto, Canada, which undertook several laboratory experiments designed to investigate claims of "pyramid power." It is her view, and that of her husband, Dr. A. R. G. Owen, Professor of Mathematics, University of Toronto, that their experiments are unique, because controlled laboratory tests of the effects of pyramid shapes have not been undertaken elsewhere on the same level of strict scrutiny. Professor Owen, director of the foundation, is a parapsychological researcher of long standing; his book Can We Explain the Poltergeist? *received the Treatise Award of the Parapsychology Foundation and the Duke University Laboratory Prize for distinguished work in parapsychology.*

One characteristic of "pyramidology" is the degree to which claims for "pyramid power" multiply and are exaggerated as they pass from country to country, and with the passage of time. This was amusingly illustrated during the Second World War, when the London daily paper, *The Times,* published letters to the editor over the signature of one "Colonel Musselwhite." One of the colonel's letters alleged that razor blades would give a better shave if kept on a north-south axis to pick up the earth's magnetic field. This letter did not mention pyramids at all; later, however, someone combined the "magnetic field" concept with that of pyramid power and stated that, because the Cheops Pyramid is on a direct north-south axis, razor blades kept in such a pyramid would resharpen themselves, and thus last forever.

This combination of ideas reminds me of the parlor game

that is played by whispering a sentence into the ear of the person sitting next to you in a circle, who then tells it to the next person, and so on, until it comes back to you—usually hilariously distorted and bearing little or no resemblance to the original sentence. In the case of the dramatic north-south razor blade claim, "Colonel Musselwhite" was later revealed as a pseudonym of Professor R. V. Jones, Department of Physics, Aberdeen University, Scotland. Jones, an eminent scientist with a taste for practical jokes, once lectured to the institute of Physics on "The Theory of Practical Joking; Its Relevance to Physics." During the war, Jones served the British Ministry of Defence. One of his hoaxes tricked 400 German bombers off their paths; another prompted the German navy to coat its submarines with anti-infrared paint.

When we began research into "pyramid power" at the New Horizons Research Foundation in 1971, only two major claims were made by its proponents. Since then, what we might call the "Musselwhite Effect" of expanded and distorted claims has overtaken the original ideas, which had been limited as follows: that organic material, such as meat, eggs, and fish, when placed inside a pyramid built to the proportions of the Cheops Pyramid, and placed on a level one third of the way from the base, would be preserved for a longer period than the same kind of material would be outside the pyramid. Proponents of this theory differed as to whether the pyramid should be pointed to the true north or the magnetic north; this is a difference of a few degrees, although each claimant states that it is important to be exact! Concurrently, it was stated that razor blades placed inside the pyramid would resharpen themselves and last indefinitely. As there seemed to be no scientific reason why a pyramid shape should have this effect, we decided to investigate this claim ourselves. We could find no accounts of scientific experiments that proved these claims.

In April, 1972, we carried out a series of experiments with a team of researchers headed by Allen Alter and Dale Simmons. We built cardboard pyramids to the specifications said to reproduce the proportions of the Cheops Pyramid, and we bought commercial pyramids of the same size. The test materials used were hamburger, meat, potato, bean sprouts, banana, apple, liver, and bone marrow. In all cases the test material was supported on a rigid platform of thin cardboard and placed with its center below the apex of the pyramid, which was oriented to the true north. Bean sprouts were laid in a small bunch, randomly oriented on the platform. Specimens of other material were used in slices ¼ inch thick, laid horizontally on the platform. Whenever the specimen was other than circular (as it was with bananas), the major axis was aligned to true north. The experiments were first done with the top of the platform at the one-third level. They were repeated with the specimens at various other levels, one half, three fourths, etc. and also with the specimens in the bottom right-hand corner. Specimens were inspected at forty-eight-hour intervals over a period of two weeks.

In each experiment, a specimen of test material—as similar as possible in composition, dimension, and age to that in the pyramid—was placed in each of various-shaped cardboard containers, of volume equal to the pyramid, in the forms of rectangular parallelopipeds, cubes, triangular prisms, and cones. This use of control groups seems to have been omitted in testing done by other groups.

In all tests, the members of the research team, who performed their experiments independently in their various homes and offices, while following the same agreed protocols, were quite unable to discover any significant differences between material placed in a pyramid and material placed in the control containers. If anything, we had only rediscovered the "Cookie-Jar Principle"; that is, any substance placed in a container that keeps out air currents does not spoil as quickly as it would in the open air.

Specifically, we learned that hamburger and steak were bad test materials. A butcher explained to us that most commercial hamburger has preservatives added to it to prevent rotting, and good steak meat can be left at room temperature on a kitchen table for one week and still be good enough to eat.

Potatoes at first appeared to show less deterioration under a pyramid than in the other containers; but when the test was repeated with more care, no difference could be recorded. The explanation appeared to be that one slice of potato was somewhat thicker than the others. When care was taken to make all slices of equal quarter-inch thickness, there were no detectable differences. Results with apples and bean sprouts were also identical whether pyramids or other containers were used. Notably, bean sprouts are the easiest material to work with as they dry out within twelve hours.

The tests with bananas carried out at various levels within the pyramid gave typical results as follows:

In the bottom north corner; some light areas, not completely sticky.

Halfway up; more light areas than in the north corner, not completely sticky.

Quarter way up; some light areas, very sticky.

Control (in open air); dried out and sticky.

In the cases of liver and bone marrow, control and pyramid specimens were tested twice: oriented to the magnetic north pole and then oriented to true north. In every case, results were basically the same; the liver was hard and shiny with only slight odor; in the marrow samples, there was no odor or change of color.

As a separate experiment, potato slices were tested at different phases of the moon. Again, no difference could be detected.

Our group concluded that though, for all that is known to the contrary, there may be a mysterious force within the Great Pyramid itself, our investigations do not support the proponents of the theory that anyone can produce this effect in a model pyramid in their own home.

The preservation properties alleged to be possessed by the pyramids may, in fact, be due to the climate in which the Egyptian pyramids are located. Dry desert air is notoriously preservative. In the desert areas of Peru, which we have visited, the preservation of Inca corpses in the museums is remarkable; their clothing looks as fresh as if woven recently. The air there is very dry, and these bodies were buried in sand graves. The latest theory about the preservation of Egyptian mummies is that they were preserved not as a result of special embalming methods, but because of the climate in which they were buried. And, of course, the majority of the mummies found in Egypt were *not* found in pyramids!

There was an interesting criminal case in England some ten years ago. In a seaside resort on the North Wales coast, a murderer was convicted of a crime he had committed several years previously. The criminal had murdered an old lady and hung her body in a closet on the landing of the boarding house which he owned. He then locked the closet, and left the neighborhood, leaving instructions that the closet was not to be opened, as it contained his personal belongings. Some years later, new tenants, curious as to the contents of the closet, forced it open, to find the body of the old lady, hanging in a perfect state of preservation. Autopsy determined the cause of her death and led to the apprehension of her murderer. The evidence consisted of a great deal of expert testimony to the effect that hanging in a cool dry closet (there was a hole in the back that allowed a draft of air) had produced mummification. There had been no putre-faction, no decay, and no smell. The local newspaper labeled the court proceedings, "The Mummy Murder Trial."

Our Toronto group tested the theory that razor blades were resharpened by keeping them in a pyramid shape. We also tested the theory that flowers could be preserved. The experiments with the razor blades were performed in a metal-lurgical laboratory at Ryerson Polytechnic Institute, Toronto, with the aid of a metallurgical microscope and Polaroid Instamatic camera combination. Two types of pyramid were used, one a commercially manufactured pyramid, and one constructed by the group according to the specifications in the Ostrander and Schroeder book.

The pyramids were oriented to the magnetic north, with a platform one third of the height of the pyramid situated directly under the apex. During the experiment, the pyramids were situated on the top shelf of a closet away from sources of temperature variation and from any electronic or high-frequency generating devices.

The razor blades selected for the experiment were Gem blades of the older type, without any edge coating such as platinum or stainless steel. Three blades were used, Blade A on the platform under the commercial pyramid, Blade B on the platform under the home-built pyramid, and C in the open air as a control. Just before the experiment, each blade was dulled by ten strokes of medium pressure through the bristles of a toothbrush, and a picture was taken of its work-ing edge with the aid of the microscope-camera combination. The blades were then placed on the shelf and left undisturbed for seven days. All were oriented to magnetic north. After seven days, the blades were removed and a new photomicro-graph of the end and side of the working edge of each blade was taken. A picture was also taken of a Wilkinson Sword blade which had been used for shaving several times, as a standard of comparison to show that the blades in the experi-ment had been dulled to about the same extent as a used razor blade, but not too severely.

The photographs showed little difference, if any, in the before-and-after states of the blades. Moreover, any such slight changes as were present were mimicked by the control

blade, the one kept in the open air. All the instructions pre-
scribed for the use of pyramids were followed to the letter in
the conduct of the experiment. As an overall conclusion one
must say that the pyramids did not affect the blades in any
physical way. In all the literature we have read, regarding the
capacities of pyramids to preserve meat and resharpen razor
blades, we have found no statistical or circumstantial data
concerning experiments or control experiments. Therefore it
seems reasonable to make the following comments.

a. Subjectivity; the psychological aspect. How dull is dull
when a person considers a blade too dull to shave with? Also,
how does one tell whether a blade is really sharper or not
after it has been in a pyramid for restoration? Judgment on
these points is inevitably highly subjective and liable to ma-
nipulation by underlying wishes, desires, and expectations,
so that it cannot be equated to an assay made by a scientifically based objective method. In addition, subjective tests
of sharpness are rendered imprecise by the unquantifiable
factor of acuteness of memory, because the "before" and
"after" tests are separated by a considerable lapse of time.

b. Natural equilibrium; the homeostatic aspect. There is a
tendency in nature which, though not universal, is widespread, for things when disturbed, to return to the previous
state of equilibrium. In physics this is exemplified by Le
Chatelier's Principle, in biology by homeostasis. It has long
been known that a used razor blade tends to "feel" sharper
if used after a period of rest. This can be ascribed to the
motion of air molecules around and against the blade which
helps to wear down its weakest parts (which are, in fact, the
jagged peaks or points). Also, when a blade is used, the stress
upon its cells is changed, some being compressed and others
stretched. During a period of disuse, the forces of compres-
sion and tension will tend to restore the internal stresses to an
equilibrium state.

Since, as far as we are aware, no scientific experiment on
pyramids and razor blades has ever been published, we assume that pyramid enthusiasts, when testing their hypothesis,
have neglected to take adequate account of factors (a) and
(b), or to make adequate control experiments.

Finally, we did two experiments with fresh flowers. Four
roses were placed in different containers—one in a commercial pyramid, one in the open air, one under the home-built
pyramid, and one in a cube of volume equal to the home-built
pyramid. Each rose was placed with its center directly under

the geometrical center of the figure, the figure oriented to magnetic north. Three chrysanthemums were placed as follows: one in the open air, one in a home-built pyramid, one in a cube of equal volume to the pyramid. The experiments were set up on a closet shelf, away from temperature variations and high frequency or voltage-generating devices, and left undisturbed for seven days before being inspected. None of the roses differed appreciably in color. It was found that the roses under the pyramids were more resilient and pliable than the one which had remained in air. However, there was no difference between the roses under pyramids and the rose under the cube. The chrysanthemum which had been in the air was less brittle than those under the pyramid and the cube, but these two were in identical condition.

With the flowers, as with the razor blades, there was no effect which could be attributed directly and solely to the shape of the pyramid; such differences as there were between the enclosed and unenclosed flowers could have been due to the lack of air circulation in the cube and pyramid.

Our experiments were carefully done and carefully evaluated. We felt we had settled the "pyramid question," certainly to our own satisfaction. Our results were published, and some of the responses were quite unexpected. People wrote in to say that they were surprised that we could not "make the pyramids work"—had we discovered where we went wrong in our experiments yet? A schoolteacher friend had similar responses when he set his class to some experiments with pyramids. The reactions of his pupils were not "How interesting, we seem to have disproved the theory," but "What have we done wrong—we can't make it work." We received a good deal of correspondence arguing the virtues of the magnetic north, or the true north, and pyramidologists are fairly evenly divided on this. Equally, these same people will allege that a deflection of the smallest amount of degree will destroy the results. Yet both sides claim infallible results with their own orientation.

Since our experiments, the fad has burgeoned further. Now, the claims are wilder. It is claimed that if a person sits in a pyramid for a period of time, or sleeps in it, he will become calmer, more relaxed, and be a better person able to meditate better. Also children will grow—despite the fact that other claims regarding preservation of meat involve killing growing things, namely bacteria! Where pyramids with open sides, made of wire, are placed over growing plants, they are alleged to increase the plants' growth. Biological experiments of this nature are very difficult to conduct and evaluate —factors such as identical growing conditions, moisture, air, sunlight, as well as the difficulty of getting identical plants (even peas in one pod produce different size plants) have to be overcome to produce a properly scientific experiment. However, neither buyer nor seller in this market appears to be overly critical. One enthusiastic exponent of pyramid power, when asked to explain how he got his results (obviously very much better plants under his wire pyramids than the ones in the open), naïvely explained, "Well, I set a row of seeds, and as the first ones come up, I pop a pyramid over them." Since, naturally, the healthiest and strongest plants come up first, he is determining the result of his experiment from the beginning! Another enthusiast, disturbed by our razor blade experiment, went to great lengths to explain to us that by dulling the blades by cutting a toothbrush we were doing it all wrong—his theory was that the pyramid dissolves the soap and grease accumulated on the blade when shaving; this is what makes the blade dull! A totally new explanation and quite different from the earlier ones.

If the results of our experiments suggest a negative element, that is merely the inevitable conclusion one must draw from the data that has emerged. However, as experimenters we remain open to new ideas; we would be curious to know of other attempts at replications that differ from our own and generally feel that our own personal and scientific curiosity makes us receptive to open-minded evaluation of all claims for positive results in pyramid studies and related areas.

Pyramids, Western Style

by Wanda Sue Childress

From France to Czechoslovakia to Arizona and all of the American Southwest—that is the voyage pyramid power has made in a few years. Ms. Childress, who lives in Tempe, Arizona, reports on pyramidologists in this area. She notes that adherents to a wide variety of occult ideas, from those who seek contact with Unidentified Flying Objects (UFO) to members of religious cults, have taken up the pyramid fad. The result is a patchwork of ideas, people, and structures, of claims and hopes and enthusiasms.

Do sex, magic, and pyramids mix? "Indeed," says Roger X., high priest of a witchcraft coven in the Greater Phoenix area. "But we call it Magick. We gather, both men and women, nude. There's power in the pyramid that enhances sex energy. We do healing, develop ESP, and gain control of our lives through Sex Magick. It's not an orgy. It's not black magic. It's white. It's used to help us and others."

Nearby, in the west side of Phoenix, a stately pyramid rises at Asbury Methodist Church. Unlike the usual four-sided triangular pyramid, the chapel where the Reverend Paul Wilkinson gives the Order for the Administration of the Sacrament of the Lord's Supper, or Holy Communion, is octagonal. The chapel expands from its bases outward, reaching four feet, or one fourth of their height in expansion. The chapel is thirty-six feet high (from base to dome) and thirty-six feet across at its broadest point.

The silence within the chapel rings. Even more unusual, the Reverend Wilkinson himself appears to ring. From his body emanates a high-pitched humming sound, like a single note, possibly because Reverend Wilkinson practices a unique form of exercise: active meditation designed to infuse every bodily zone with a vital spiritual force that amplifies his cells' sounds.

Paul Wilkinson is a cabala expert, who practices what he teaches others: vitalizing your own tree of life, the body, in order to "be a perfect androgyne." He explains that "an androgyne is a person in whom both male and female aspects are perfectly balanced." Such balance brings about a state of fullness within self, in which the "glow-ry" of God shines in one's own spirituality. It can often be seen as the glow around healers, perceptible to persons whose sensitivity is highly developed.

Paul Wilkinson performs the sacraments early every Sunday morning in the "pyramid," which he calls the Chapel of the Beatitudes. Many healings are reported to occur therein. I was present when a woman, who suffered bursitis of the left arm so badly she was in constant pain, was healed thirty seconds after stepping into the exact middle of the chapel. She had not come to church to be healed and was more surprised than Paul when, suddenly, all pain vanished. Paul Wilkinson believes in Divine Energy. He has witnessed its presence in others and in himself.

Energy—pyramid style—is a post-1970 phenomenon. The quest for pyramid power is on!" "People meditate inside pyramids, sharpen carbon-steel razor blades in them, store food in them, and even send long-distance thoughts through pyramid-like crystals or triangular-shaped rocks. Much of this pioneer pyramiding is taking place in the American West.

People wishing to see an Egyptian influence in art and artifacts must visit San Jose, California, where the Rosicrucian Order (AMORC) maintains its Egyptian Museum. It contains many original Egyptian treasures, plus some excellent reproductions of Egyptian statuary, artifacts, and architecture. Interior settings in the museum and the Order's headquarters are reminiscent of the pyramids as they may have appeared during the height of the Ancient Egyptian culture nearly 5,000 years ago.

The most popular concept of "pyramid" is a four-sided structure containing four equal triangle sides. American architecture features a variety of non-Egyptian style pyramids, primarily those created with stair-step sides and even arched or flat roofs. Pyramids of antiquity remain a mystery to modern man.

Pyramid-hunters, a new breed of American, journey south to the Pyramid of the Niches in El Tajín, Veracruz, Mexico. This Totonac Indian pyramid was discovered in heavy jungle. Excavations revealed a duplicate structure inside the outer pyramid.

Around its sides, the sixty-foot-high outer pyramid contains 365 niches, one for each day of a solar year. Evidently it served as a calendar. Lesser Tajín contains inscriptions of crosses, swastikas, and even some Greek and Roman sculpture. The Totonac civilization was destroyed by the Aztecs at the time of the Spanish conquest, but the origin of the pyramids—or of those who inspired their building—remains a mystery.

Pyramid-hunters also travel north, to Arizona's Verde River Valley area in the center of the state. There they visit Tuzigoot, site of Pueblo Indian ruins dating back as far as the year 1150 A.D. This pueblo, built atop a hill, looks like a giant pyramid from the distance. Actually, it was an adobe architectural feat of communal living. Two stories high, the structure contained approximately eighty-nine ground-floor and twenty-one second-floor rooms. Average rooms were twelve by eighteen feet. Residents entered through rooftops, after climbing ladders to their quarters. The site was excavated by the University of Arizona in 1933–34. It is believed the Pueblo Indians had left the valley long before Antonio Espejo and his Spanish soldiers arrived in 1583.

Although the Arizona State Historical Society says no known ancient pyramids exist in Arizona, I found plenty of modern pyramids in Arizona, some reduced to the size of stones in jewelry. Serious seekers of pyramid power, in fact, frequently find crystals and pyramids inextricably woven. This combination made one young couple in Scottsdale, Arizona, rich. Teaming pyramid power with superstition, they set crystals or other triangular-shaped rocks from Arizona soil into silver rings, bracelets, or necklaces, and labeled them "demon-chasers." Little handwritten cards accompanied the displays of jewelry. In essence, potential buyers were told that the effectiveness of this jewelry, which looked like the jewelry dozens of other young jewelers were peddling to tourists, lay in its power to chase away demons.

Whether the demons were one's own thoughts, or spells cast by someone else, was irrelevant. People bought the jewelry because it promised to chase away "bad vibes." Most buyers of demon-chasing jewelry were college or university

students. Many of them were "into" the occult and mixed a
pyramid meditation and demon-chasing.

The American West is regarded by many to be half a
century ahead of the rest of the country in its free-thinking,
trend-setting ways. Arizona, no longer the land of desperados,
today is one of America's centers for Ufologists and pyramidologists. For one reason, contactees and leaders of the
"flying saucers are real" movement of the early 1960's have
established numerous organizations on desert sites in Arizona.
Many of them have, in fact, subjected themselves to the
discomfort—and potential poverty—of desert living because
they believe man is not alone in the cosmos, that communication with "space brothers and sisters," all part of Divine
Intelligence, is easier and more likely to occur in uncongested
open areas. Also, UFOs and alien craft could land with greater safety on the desert than elsewhere in the nation. The
"space believers" welcome extraterrestrials.

Among the best-known leaders in the space movement are
George Van Tassel, who resides at Giant Rock in the California desert; Bob Rose, who runs the Blue Rose Ministry
in Joshua Tree, California; and Dr. Daniel W. Fry, who
heads Understanding, Inc., headquartered at Tonopah, Arizona.

From San Diego north to San Francisco, and from Las
Vegas south to Phoenix, thousands of men and women from
all walks of life have joined others who confess, "I believe
in life from space." The reason: many of these people have
witnessed unidentified aerial phenomena.

Psychics frequently claim communication with "space people" and mediums appear at gatherings in the Southwest
to read messages received from space—or go into a trance
and make "direct communication." The mysteries of life are
prime subjects of discussion, often including "answers" to the
mysteries of the Great Pyramid of Gizeh, or the Pyramid
of Cheops.

Every UFO buff in the American West knows who Kla-la
is. Whether or not they really believe in Kla-la is their business, but selling Kla-la to the people *is* business for Polaris
Foundation's Solar Cross Library in Phoenix. Kla-la is an
electronic voice that sounds very human, very male, and
speaks on a tape entitled: *"The Great Pyramid."* It says:

"Greetings. I am Kla-la . . . In the beginning, approximately 45,600 years before your Christ . . . survey ships of
the Confederation wanted to establish an outpost . . . upon

your planet Earth. The crews from the third planet . . . approached your planet and started construction on what is known in your day as the Great Pyramid. Huge blocks of the substance . . . were quarried from the continent . . . and brought by our craft . . . to your present location. Huge disc rays cut and sliced and shaped these blocks . . . In that edifice known as the Great Pyramid were laid generators totaling millions of watts of energy . . . Noticing the tremendous impact this structure had . . . on the natives . . . it was felt that subsidiary functions could be included . . . Also, at that time it was felt desirable to place observation teams of our people upon your planet to check the rates of progress of various races, to help in establishing more even distribution . . . Your scientific circles find evidence of many types of flora and fauna scattered throughout many portions of your globe . . ."

The voice fades and is then clearly audible again, explaining that those setting forth in their starships and regularly visiting earth could see "the need of cultures yet to be born. Certain influences were to be in order . . . These were placed in the pyramid. A shaft deeply built by subterranean chamber, there the mightiest generators of the race . . . were installed . . . in which my brothers function to this day . . ."

The voice continues: "Khufu or Cheops much later, puzzling at this spectacle, decided that such a monument should be established . . . thousands of the native population were set to work and slabs and blocks of lime were built up around our edifice and now . . . peculiar metal adorned the top . . . they decided to let it shine forth, for it could be seen by travelers many miles away. This is why your ancient Grecian writers thought it to be a fact that Khufu was the one who erected the pyramid . . . Unknown to your people, regular crews of our people manned the equipment . . . The Queen's Chamber was primarily an interstellar communications room. The King's Chamber was later installed. This chamber was established for heating . . . Our people, under the guise of the local priests of the town, administered treatment that many believed to be miracles. In this, we found an expedient way of lending aid where possible and at all times the throb of living generators worked continually, throwing radiant beams of energy into the heavens of the universe to guide our craft."

The voice, described in the excerpts from the tape above, summarizes dimensions of the pyramid, concluding with the statement: "Nine is the key to the mathematical science dealing with magnetics. It has been my privilege to speak. I am Kla-la."

Kla-la claims huge blocks of lime were quarried from earth, and thousands of the native population were set to work; but I have also heard a very different "psychic" version of the pyramid-building process of the mysterious Egyptian past. The following is typical:

"The ancient Egyptians didn't drag heavy rock across the desert and thousands of people didn't work like it's told! Paul Revere never took his famous ride, either. It's just not so. I was there. I know! Don't laugh. I lived before. The Egyptians knew the secret to creating those stones from available materials right on the desert. They worked with what you call gravity. Gravity does not pull down. Air pushes down, then rises back up. They worked with the energy in the air. They made the stones lighter than air or the same weight, then lifted them on rising energy.

"They knew the secret, that in the exact center of each stone is an area that is weightless. They used pulleys on that exact spot. They just lifted the stones and put 'em into place. It's no big secret. Man can do the same thing today."

This statement did not come from a trained psychic or scientific investigator, but from a six-year-old boy who had no education in ancient history and no background in science. This illustrates the "variant" information on a related subject received psychically. It is little wonder that science often scoffs at material received intuitively, particularly if psychics attach price tags to their prophecies.

Primarily, man lives in a three-dimensional world, a world of breadth, depth, and height. These factors are measurable and calculable. The pyramid form fits into this three-dimensional reality. It is, however, the fourth dimension of the pyramid that holds man's mind in fascination. This dimension is simply the "power" inside, perhaps also outside, the actual pyramidal structure. In order to experience pyramid power, most people must first experience a physical pyramid. I have encountered a few exceptions to this rule—but very few.

In the American Southwest there exist a handful of men and women who have literally lived by metaphysical principles most of their adult lives. Generally, they do not make public displays of their abilities, yet they claim to control matter by using the power of their minds to create their own worlds. These people walk the mainstreams of life, living and working among average American citizens. Many of this small group are Rosicrucians—although not all of them belong to that worldwide fraternity that claims descent from the Egyptian mystery schools. While they are highly psychic, they neither make prophets of themselves nor profits from their abilities. They use knowledge to improve their lives and thus set inspiring examples to others. They tend to be free from colds, depressions, and other contagions that afflict society in general. They are frequently prominent in the fields of culture, education, the healing arts, and science. One of their secrets is that they live daily in pyramids, which they construct about themselves merely by mentally controlling the energy in their auras, or magnetic fields.

As one of these anonymous civic leaders explained: "Each morning before getting out of bed, spend a few minutes in meditation. Create, by imagining it, a pyramid formed of white light around yourself. Its peak should be directly over your head. Its base should extend beneath your feet. Wherever you go, wherever you are, know always that you are in the center of your own four-sided pyramid. No harm can come to you. It is your veil, your protecting shield, your entryway into both the cosmos and the finite reality."

He added: "No one else, except a person like yourself, will be able to see your pyramid. But you can see it because its reality is in the eye of the beholder—its Creator. If you learn to live in a pyramid, harm will be far less likely to afflict you and good health and clear thinking and understanding will surely enlighten your days. The more endowed you become with the ability to control nature, the greater will be the power of your pyramid. The physical structure of a pyramid holds energy in motion. The psychic pyramid-builder can hold the same energy in motion without need of boards, bricks, or mortar."

If you don't want to surround yourself with an invisible pyramid, but don't want to build one—or can't find one in which to spend some time in your neighborhood—you may try the following method of benefiting from pyramid power. Sleep above a pyramid! This suggestion is shared by a man from northern California. He is George H. Wilkins of Broderick, California, who founded the Universalist Fellowship more than fifteen years ago "as a cosmic command from the Brothers of Venus represented by Sanat Kumara, Lord of Venus and Protector of Earth's evolutions for aeons." Today, in his thirties, Dr. Wilkins wears many hats. He is a hypnotherapist in Sacramento. He is a counselor. He performs psychic readings "on the side" and he produces volumes of educational material designed to help man help himself. Two major courses offered by Dr. Wilkins are "Solar Science" and "Alpha Mind—The Extra-Sensory Science." The former course, solar science, teaches students basic techniques for developing their own light bodies to become living suns (gods) in the Godhead. The latter course teaches, among other things, continuous existence on alpha brain-wave levels, with resultant ability to recall past lives.

While Dr. Wilkins sells his courses through the mail, I have personally seen him give away his teachings to students who sincerely wish to lead more spiritual lives but cannot afford financial outlays at the moment. Dr. Wilkins told me that a number of years ago he was taken aboard a craft of the type commonly called UFO. His instruction in the teachings he now shares began when he was quite young at "Lake Titicaca, where I received training with the White Brotherhood for six years in the Brotherhood of the Seven Rays there." He adds: "I consider myself a Father to humans giving birth to themselves (god-self). He is knowledgeable about pyramids, concurring with L. Turenne, author of *Mysterious Science of the Pharaohs,* and says:

"Various forms, Turenne asserts, such as spheres, pyramids, semi-spheres, and squares act as different types of resonators for the energy of the cosmos, the sun, and the energy all around us. Just as the special shape of a violin gives tone and quality to a bow touching a string . . . the special shape of a pyramid apparently is a resonant cavity for the 'live' crystals of a razor blade (animate matter) and recharges (rejuvenates) same to last up to ten times longer while kept in a pyramid."

Dr. Wilkins says further, "While I'm not at liberty to give the Cosmic Godhood knowledge, the angling of physical atoms to a ninety-degree phase-shift formula may be made public by you." Dr. Wilkins wants the resonator shown below to be shared with readers. He advises: "Obtain an inexpensive compass of plastic material, available at auto stores. Determine due north; place the pyramid resonator under your bed and point one of the corners due north for suggested benefit of spirituality, physical regeneration, rejuvenation, healing and spiritual integration of all psychic bodies."

Place the generator—which can be made of paper or

plastic—directly under the portion of the bed where you sleep.

While esoterica, such as invisible pyramid auras or under-the-bed pyramid resonators, might work for some persons, the average pyramid experimenter sticks with conventional three-dimensional structures: height, breadth, and depth.

The most popular in modern America is the pyramid constructed in mathematical ratios paralleling the dimensional scale of the Great Pyramid. For a six-inch pyramid, the base of each of the four triangle sides should be 9⅜ inches; the sides should be 8⅞ inches. By converting inches to feet, a pyramid-builder can make a six-foot-high pyramid. By doubling all dimensions, he will make a twelve-foot-high pyramid, and by tripling dimensions he will create an eighteen-foot-high pyramid.

A popular variation on the Cheops model theme is the American pyramid built with seven feet of side (height) for every eleven feet of base (width), creating a pyramid that is actually shorter but broader than the Cheops model. It has long been believed that seven-eleven is a lucky numerical combination. Geometrically, it is a balanced combination. Scientifically, the energy generated in a pyramid according to those angles is still under investigation.

Pyramids in both the Cheops and seven-eleven styles can be found throughout the West. A lady near Apache Junction, Arizona, built a small pyramid from chicken wire and plaster. It failed to please her aesthetic taste, and she left it in the yard. A stray dog was attracted into the structure and gave birth to eleven pups.

A group of children in California made a pyramid from old bedsheets. They hung the sheets on the clothesline, forming the apex, and secured the sides with clothespins. They held the base in place with rocks. After camping out for several nights in the pyramid tent, they reported "strange dreams" and "the feeling something weird was in the tent." One night a stray raccoon entered the tent.

A sixth-grade class in a private, progressive parochial school in Arizona built a pyramid in the classroom, using old cardboard boxes secured with masking tape. One afternoon the mother superior, making the rounds of the classrooms, entered this particular room. Noting that the class was rather sparse, she made an investigation. Several sixth-grade boys had fallen asleep inside the pyramid. The teacher was reprimanded and the pyramid put into the trash bins of a nearby

Pyramid Resonator

Cut two resonator sides per dimensions given
on bottom diagram, using cardboard or plastic.

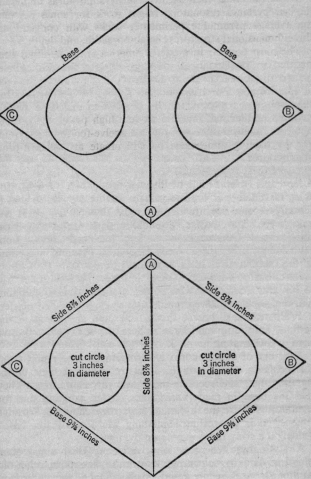

Tape sides together from points A to B.
Fold center lines.
Tape sides together from points A to C.
Align one point of pyramid with north.

Suggest placing under bed directly beneath spot where you sleep.

market—from whence it originally came. The nun's comment was, "This is an educational institution, not a movie set for rehearsals of *Auntie Mame*."

A schoolteacher from Glendale, Arizona, hangs a plastic pyramid tent from the chandelier in her den. Guests sit in the pyramid, drinking wine and witnessing a "light show" projected onto the sides of the tent from a revolving light fixture in the center of the pyramid. Gregorian chants played on tape add to the atmosphere.

The Greater Phoenix area, called the Valley of the Sun, is the nucleus of a psychic boom—hundreds of "fortune tellers" practice as licensed psychics or as ministers of unorthodox religions. Centers and associations and churches—all teaching psychical development and correlated spiritual growth—are found in Arizona. Pyramid power has found its way into many of these movements.

Bob and Helen Doyle of Phoenix are known for their aura mirrors. These mirrors are said to enable people to look at themselves and see their own auric emanations with the naked eye. The Doyles, an affable pair who teach metaphysics in their home, place aura mirrors under model pyramids before using them. Andy Ghigo, another popular leader in the metaphysical truth movement of Arizona, runs an insurance business from his Glendale home. He built a pyramid in his yard, complete with sound and color. Numerous remarkable healings have been reported.

William and Elizabeth Finch, founders of Esoteric Publications, hold an annual Psychic Seminar in Phoenix. Its purpose is dissemination of knowledge and demonstration of natural but often paranormal principles—the only profit motive being to enrich people's lives by enriching their understanding. In March, 1975, the historic "firewalk" which made the *Guinness Book of World Records* was performed at the seminar by Vernon E. Craig, cheesemaker from Wooster, Ohio, who is known professionally as "Komar, the Hindu Fakir."

The Finches live in Sedona, Arizona. They are pioneer experimenters in a process they call photochromotherapy. Author David St. Clair described the Finches' works in *How Your Psychic Powers Can Make You Rich:* "They have long been aware that certain colors heal a wound faster than ordinary white light. When red was shone on a body, circulation was improved. Yellow, played upon the body of a diabetic, somehow helped him with his insulin problem."

The Finches were intrigued by the primitive belief that "if you take a photograph of someone, you also take part of their soul," according to St. Clair, who adds, "They also know many mediums who deal with psychometry. These mediums take a photograph of a person and by holding it are able to get the vibrations and tell quite a bit about this person's personality, and often even their physical illnesses."

Bill and Elizabeth Finch decided to experiment. If it was true that colors had a healing effect and photos were extensions of the soul, then color played upon photos might help heal persons, even those who were at great distances. They invented a box containing colored lights. A photo was placed in this box and light/color played upon it. Many cases of healing were reported, including a man who recovered from cataracts and a dog that recovered from an infection of the tail.

Elizabeth Finch told me, "We have never had time to really research pyramid power. The only use we have made of it has been in our Chromolight units; the space that holds the photograph is lined with a material that contains a multitude of tiny pyramids. We feel this might multiply the energy of the colors, but have never established much factual data, as the colors seem to work so well even without the pyramid filters."

Basically, the primary colors you might want to experiment with if you build a pyramid, are:

COLOR	EFFECTS
Red	Stimulator. Increases circulation. Rouses aggressive impulses, makes you feel more fear-free. Can be sexually stimulating. An energy builder.
Blue	A peaceful relaxer. Inspirational. Stimulates creative thought and expression. Turns energy toward the inner, less aggressive but mentally active person inside you. Good color for falling asleep by.
Yellow	A mental, clear color. Helps to clear the mind and stimulate, yet relax, the body; put thoughts in order.

You may use colored light bulbs in a large pyramid in which you meditate. Or you might want to place a small Christmas tree light bulb in a six-inch model pyramid you build, placing a photograph of a person to be healed directly beneath it in the center of the pyramid.

As you have seen, people are building pyramids out of every conceivable material—from plastic sheets to boards to bed sheets. The pyramid built by Dr. Daniel W. Fry and his wife, Florence Durfee Fry, R.N., at Tonopah, Arizona, is a good example of popular modern pyramidal structure. I have selected this pyramid as an example of do-it-yourself craftsmanship because it features durable materials that are relatively inexpensive.*

The base of the pyramid is approximately sixteen feet wide, with the height of the four triangles' sides being twelve feet. A corner of the pyramid faces north. A crawl space facing northeast allows visitors to climb into the pyramid. A hanging door then closes to shut out light.

The Frys' pyramid has a floor which has been carpeted with soft, tufted green wall-to-wall pile. Inner walls have been paneled to create a space between the outer wall and the interior. This provides storage room for foods. Overhead, directly under the apex of the pyramid, on the inside ceiling wall, an air vent has been installed. No electronic cooling system operates in the Fry pyramid, yet even on blistering days on the desert the ambient temperature inside the pyramid is relatively cool.

Six people can sit in meditative poses comfortably. Eight people can fit in the structure at one time, but the sensation is one of being crowded with this many people. Dan Fry recommends to visitors, "We suggest you limit your visit to no longer than one hour. The pyramid was built for research, experimentation, and storage of food. The management makes no claims or takes no responsibility for any effects on the visitor."

The most unusual experience I had while researching in this field happened in conjunction with two visits to Dan and Florence Fry's pyramid. I cannot explain the experience. It was, to put it mildly, mind-boggling. Here, as briefly as possible, is that experience:

Friday, May 17, 1975: I decided to wear a blue cardboard

---

*Fiberboard and wood are the principal materials used, with carpeting adding an element of luxury and comfort.

triangle on the string bearing my Egyptian scarab into Dr. Dan W. Fry's pyramid. Dr. George H. Wilkins of Universalist Fellowship had given me this cardboard triangle, about three inches in height, and a cardboard circle about three inches in diameter. I placed the cardboard triangle on a string by poking the string through a hole in the top of the triangle. My cousin Margaret Runyan Castaneda witnessed me take the string and hang it around my neck, tucking the triangle and scarab into my bra. I left the cardboard circle, which also had holes punched in it, lying by the fishbowl on my coffee table.

Saturday, May 18, 1975: I had slept all night with the string around my neck. I arose, dressed, and left for Tonopah at 6:30 A.M., arriving at around 9 A.M. In the early afternoon I visited the Frys' pyramid with a few other women guests at Understanding, Inc. Meditation was impossible because every stray housefly between Phoenix and Los Angeles seemed to have gotten into the pyramid before us. These pests kept dive-bombing at my nose, eyes, and ears. After about half an hour of frustration, I gave up attempts at meditation and left the pyramid. Attila Gavalya, my friend from Gila Bend, took me driving. We visited an abandoned dam. On the way back to Dan's and Florence's for dinner, a runaway truck nearly forced us into a ditch. I reached spontaneously for Attila's hand; suddenly our truck seemed to fly and we passed the oncoming vehicle without collision—miraculously passing without either vehicle being forced into a ditch on a very narrow country road. Attila said, "There's power in your hand."

We sat up quite late, listening to Dan talk about his encounter with extraterrestrials, as written in his book *The White Sands Incident.* Then I went to bed, not bothering to take off my clothes. The string and triangle, I believed, were still stuck in my bra.

Sunday, May 19, 1975: I woke with painful throbbing in my ears. My brain felt as if hundreds of people were in my eardrums, screaming. I could see brilliant white light. Then, before opening my eyes, I saw the round house where I had been sleeping underneath me! From the point in space it looked like a typical flying saucer photo. Instantly I descended into the central skylight, felt myself drawn down the hallway into my room and into my body! I had experienced out-of-body projection. But the sounds were still ripping my senses. I opened my eyes, plugged my ears, and realized the "noises" came from a small group of people breakfasting in the kitchen at the other end of the building.

No one was shouting. They were talking in normal voices. But my perception was so heightened I was forced to put ear plugs in my ears before joining them. Even so, the vibrations of their voices were so magnified in my head that I had to go sit outside on the porch.

Attila joined me, and after about half an hour my senses returned to normal. We then went to the pyramid to try meditating again. A woman, who told us she was a minister from New Mexico, sat in the pyramid for a few minutes. "I've heard it said," she observed, "that the real power of the pyramid is that of translation. It means that actual matter can be changed. I've even heard stories about the pharaohs being seen alive in the Egyptian pyramids. They become visible and then invisible again."

It sounded far-fetched. Besides, I didn't feel anything. I couldn't even meditate in the pyramid. I became more aware of my body's senses instead of less aware in the pyramid. After a few minutes, Attila and I left the pyramid.

I then went into my room. Suddenly I had the urge to take the string from around my neck. I did.

And there, where the cardboard triangle had hung, was the cardboard circle I had left (or thought I left) on my living room table.

I returned home, puzzled, and checked the table. No cardboard circle was there.

Monday, May 20, 1975: I asked my cousin, Margaret, "What did I put on the string before I went to Tonopah?" She said, "I saw you put a cardboard triangle on the string."

I went to check the string, now bearing the circle, to show Margaret. The string and scarab were there, but now the circle was gone!

Tuesday, August 12, 1975: While doing my laundry I had a sudden urge to reach to a top shelf and pull down an old sack of broken hardware. I had brought it from California a year earlier and had never opened it. Now I opened the sack. There, on top of broken bits of porcelain, wire, and screws lay the blue cardboard triangle.

Saturday, October 11, 1975: When I was typing this manuscript, I opened a small envelope of research material under the heading "Wilkins" and found, to my surprise, the missing cardboard circle. It had mysteriously returned to the file

containing material from the source from whence it originally came.

Dr. Wilkins might explain, "It got lost in the ethers," but I
can only ask, "Did I experience transmutation because of
pyramid energy? Or was my mind playing colossal tricks on
me?"

During this research, I have experienced pyramids of every
conceivable type—invisible ones as well as visible ones. It is
the visible, solid, very real pyramids in America that stand as
the real proof that pyramid power is definitely creating an
influence in our lives.

Architectural styles have always been a social statement
about cultures of the times. Architecture remains as a monument to its creator's mind long after that mind has passed
into the proverbial ethers. And while it may be a century or
more before the pyramid—as a conventional form of architecture—creates a new type of city skyline, this ancient
architectural style is making a definite comeback.

A-frame homes have long been popular among southwestern artists, writers, and musicians. These homes consist of two
triangles (front and back) with roof-sides angling to the
base. Until recently, no correlation was made between pyramid power and the modified-pyramidal appearance of these
homes—many of which are found throughout Hollywood,
mecca of creative men and women in America.

Is it possible that the A-frame structure, while being pleas-
ing to the creative eye, also generates an atmosphere in
which greater creativity is engendered in the occupant's mind?
Persons who work in noncreative jobs seldom prefer A-frame
homes, except on weekends or vacations in the mountains or
at the ocean, when their minds relax. Then, perhaps, the less
conventional part of their mind becomes dominant and the
ambience of the A-frame is regenerating to their spirits.

The popular trend toward pyramid living has created spe-
cialists in pyramid construction, such as Walt Beltis, President, Bob Miller, Vice-President and Stan Elliott, Vice-
President of Cheops Corporation of Campbell, California.
This firm offers four sets of blueprints for unique pyramid
homes. They are named:

Pharaoh Seti—this is a 750-square-foot, one-bedroom
home with a high sloped-ceilinged living room, glamorized by
a ladder leading to a sumptuous 240-square-foot loft. One
side of the house branches horizontally into a carport. The
home is two-story. Plans: $115.

Pharaoh Cheops—This is a 1,560-square-foot, award-winning, three-bedroom plan with separate semi-pyramid garage. Looking like a slightly modified version of the Pyramid of Gizeh (windows and a three-tiered "capstone" are added), this model features a spiral staircase leading to two upstairs bedrooms, shower, and vanity area. Plans: $135.

Pharaoh Ramses—this is a 2,050-square-foot, three-bedroom, two-bath, family-room home with separate full-pyramid garage. The garage, two-story like the home, features a separate loft. Interior contains rough-hewn ceiling beams in family room and sun-splashed kitchen. Plans: $150.

Pharaoh Tut—this is a 1,520-square-foot, two-bedroom home with separate garage with loft. It is a complete pyramid, from tip to base, unlike other models in this group which rise pyramidally from conventional rectangular bases. Plans: $125.

Roof-walls of all four Cheops homes are covered with wood, appearing like "shake" or "shingle" exteriors. According to Cheops Corporation, "The plans follow as near to scale the dimensions of the 'Great Pyramid' of Egypt, otherwise known as Cheops Pyramid. The idea of designing a home that is consistent with the shape of a pyramid was born after many hours of laborious research. This took us into the pure and applied sciences, as well as into areas not so readily explained by current scientific methodologies, that being psychoenergy. Psycho-energy, as we learned, does exist."

While Terri Beltis of Cheops Corporation replied to my question, "Have owners of such homes reported unusual healings or other psychic or spiritual effects?" by saying, "We cannot comment on this," Cheops Corporation does state:

"Researchers do not yet know exactly what is taking place within the pyramid shape, but it is believed by many that the unique dimensions and slope of angle cause an accumulation of this mysterious energy. It is, of course, not our intention to intimate that if you were to reside in a pyramid home miracles would in fact occur, but merely to show that there is something else involved in the choice of a pyramid home. We feel that our end product is one that reflects the changing times in terms of inherent structural stability, livability and overall quality . . . You should think of everything when building a home."

People are, apparently, thinking "pyramids."

Pyramid-dwellers are on their way. In Kachimak Bay, Alaska, Elmer and Shirley Daarud live in a fifty-foot square two-story pyramid home. Its frame is wood; its walls are covered with Arizona sandstone. In 1972, in Naples, Florida, the Reverend Ronald Oesterbo and Mrs. Rose Stephans were given permission to dwell for thirty days in a plywood pyramid, after county health department officials were assured that a chemical toilet similar to those used in construction sites would be installed. And the experience of psychic researcher, Tenny Hale of Beaverton, Oregon, who attempted to erect a pyramid, reads like fiction. She was "inspired" to build a pyramid "before June, 1973." Because such a project would take money, Lazuli Productions, "for Tenny Hale," solicited funds. Ms. Hale continued to keep contributors informed on the progress of the pyramid(s), a large and small one.

Lumber and other supplies for two pyramids were slow in coming, but eventually Ms. Hale was successful in getting the pyramids completed. In February, 1974, she wrote:

"The pyramid is too cold to go into these days and the weatherstripping failed us and a great deal of moisture has gotten on the inside floor of both pyramids. I am waiting to see if the mold will grow.

"The little pyramid was put on a pickup last month . . . to be taken to the TV station [Gerry Pratt's "Watch Something Happen," KATU-TV] but then at the last minute the station decided not to bring it in. It was left on the truck while I went in to broadcast. The neighbor who loaned us the truck decided to unload it in our absence and he unhappily got stuck in the mud of our yard and the pyramid went sailing off and broke into pieces."

Ms. Hale claims she received orders to build the large pyramid "by cosmic instruction" on the seventh day of Lenten fasting during 1973. For a year she worked to achieve the goal she believed in, two pyramids—one large and one small —in which experiments could be performed that might benefit mankind by adding to the storehouse of human knowledge. The unexpected "smashing" end of the little pyramid was typical of many human dreams that end in the proverbial mud—especially among people involved in psychic research.

Scientific research is often funded by corporations, grants in aid, or universities where the work is being done. Psychics' research is most often funded by the psychics themselves or small groups of people who make contributions; yet one Arizona psychic told me, "We are part of the rest of the world when it comes to eating and paying our bills. But when it comes to making a living from the work we believe in, the rest of the world tries to push us into a corner. We don't have individual pyramids for one reason. Those who want them cannot afford them. So we all pitch in a few bucks and build one in someone's yard, so we can all use it. And what happens? The neighbors complain that it's an eyesore and the age-old battle continues."

Pyramid power is free. It's the pyramids themselves that cost money. I respect everyone who sincerely experiments with ways and means of leading a healthier, happier life— and whose sincere goal is sharing knowledge with others. The man who sold demon-chaser jewelry last year might be the man who discovers a cure to a dread disease, using pyramid power, next year. And the scientist who currently denies psychic phenomena today might be the nation's next prophet —after pyramid power works on his own psyche. Everyone is entitled to experiment with pyramids, and everyone is entitled to the benefits of this mysterious force.

Current evidence shows that the majority of pyramids in America's future will be little ones: people will wear pyramids, carry small model pyramids with them, erect miniature pyramids in their homes for razor-blade-sharpening, food storage, etc., construct pyramids large enough to sit in for meditation, or wear pyramid crystals in rings or pendants.

But the pyramids that will catch the eye of the world will be the multimillion-dollar structures that help change America's skyline into a vision of twenty-first-century space-age achievement.

Even the pharaohs who passed their monolithic limestone masterpieces on to posterity would be awed by the forthcoming pyramids and modified pyramids—not because the form is unique but because the materials used will shimmer and shine, as mirrors, testifying that man is, perhaps, ready to pass from third-dimensional living into that most mysterious realm of all—the fourth dimension.

Tomorrow's crystal-like pyramids will be made of glass. The architects designing tomorrow's gigantic pyramids will be men and women who inscribe man's evolvement scientifically, mentally, psychically, and spiritually in monuments that will be functional as well as powerful. These designers, tomorrow's pyramid-builders, will be visionary scientists.

Evidence of their arrival is here, right now. Pyramids, it is assumed, were built from the base up in ancient times.

Visitors to the beautiful Century Building in San Antonio, Texas, will recognize the base of a pyramid—done as a four-story office building approximately 100 feet by 600 feet, with facades of sloping gold glass. The architectural firm which designed the Century Building, Neuhaus & Taylor, is engaged in a similar project in Detroit, a thirty-two-story office building surrounded by a three-story-high sloping facade that encloses a mall.

Vertical facades of reflective glass can be seen on buildings throughout modern America. In the past quarter century, reflective glass has become an integral part of architecture—on conventional geometric rectangular structures and on buildings created in whole or partial pyramidal image. Mr. A. R. Hall, product manager for C-E Glass, division of Combustion Engineering, Inc., Pennsauken, New Jersey, discusses the "power," or effect, his company's product has in buildings such as the Century Building or the Royal Bank Plaza, Toronto. This project contains a twenty-one-story and forty-two-story triangular-shaped building whose hypotenuses are facing and parallel. The vertical facade is sawtoothed, so every office is a corner office. The Royal Bank Plaza project is 525,000 square feet of reflective gold glass. Hall says:

"Ordinary clear ¼-inch glass transmits about 90 percent of both visible and infrared spectrums. The major benefit of reflective glass such as ours is that it rejects a large portion of the solar energy, thus saving a great deal of money in the operation of the heating and air-conditioning systems. The glass allows 20 percent of the visible light spectrum to enter the building. It reflects the remaining 80 percent plus about 95 percent of the infrared spectrum."

In Arizona, solar energy is in the news. Harnessing and using solar energy is of national concern. Experiments are being done using pyramid forms for everything from "solar heat control" to transformation of apparently dry air into water. Greenhouses with hundreds of upside-down pyramid roofs may be popular in twenty-first-century farming; solar energy and heat, striking these pyramidal roofs from outside, may cause condensation inside the greenhouses to collect on the pyramid sides, then drip down and water the plants in the ground. In this way, pyramids could act as generators, transforming dry air into self-contained irrigation waters.

The pyramid signs are already present. Thus, I predict that a quarter century from now, pyramid power will be a major factor in American business—be it evidenced in architecture or in new economical methods developed for growing our foods and harnessing energies to keep America warm, cool, and productive. Children may go to school in pyramid-shaped classrooms, medicine might even utilize the pyramid for healing, and telegrams may be telepathed by crystal.

This isn't surprising, according to an elderly Phoenix businessman who made several fortunes by that mysterious success secret which he calls "pyramid magic." He says:

"The very business of keeping alive is pyramidal throughout the animal kingdom. The guy at the top, the leader, is the symbolic capstone. The bases, or four walls, support him. If he gives them a cut of his profit, they give him part of their earnings. It's true whether the capstone of the living pyramid's an ape, a bull seal, Abraham—the father of the tribe—or a female who is leader. It's true in our national and local government. The President is the capstone; if his bases support him strongly, the government is good and powerful. If the bases are weak, the capstone collapses and is replaced.

"In religion, the Pope is the capstone of the Catholic church. The minister is the capstone of the Protestant church. In education, the principal is the capstone of the school. His or her administrators, teachers, and students form the bases of his walls of the educational pyramid. The masses, or greatest number, lie at the bottom of the living pyramid's base. The capstone is that one top stone that connects them all. We've all been both capstones and bases during our lives. Man's evolvement into a civilized society was made possible because man knew, intuitively, there was security in pyramiding.

"I made money because, when I was a kid in college, I realized that if I wanted to get anywhere in life I'd have to be a capstone. I built a business around a product I invented. I had models built, which I paid for. Then I advertised for people to distribute my product. They paid for it, of course. They, in turn, advertised for salespeople to work under them. These people had territories. They sold the product, paid the distributors a cut, and the distributors paid me a cut. We all gave to each other, but I was the capstone that tied it all together.

"Man becomes a capstone by building a pyramid base around himself, or by rising to the capstone position through advancing up the bases—or through the ranks. A capstone is never permanent. Every capstone will be replaced someday. I've been a success in business where others have failed as capstones because I understand the secret of pyramid magic. The human capstone is representative of the only one real capstone, which most people call God.

"The ancient guys who built the pyramids knew what they were doing. The four sides of the triangle represent the dimensions. Breadth, depth, and height are physical dimensions. The fourth, spirit, is nonphysical. It's the fourth dimension that most men forget in business. I remembered it. That's how I managed to survive as a living pyramidal capstone rather than just being another president of the board."

According to the above statement, man himself is a living pyramid. Does today's keen interest in pyramidology—be it reflected in biocrystallography, pyramid meditation, or pyramidal architecture done in glass—indicate a new type of human? If yes, will tomorrow's pyramidal man be endowed with a new consciousness that allows him to know beyond the veil currently separating matter from the source? Will he be free to be his own symbolic capstone of self?

Architectural styles do make social and spiritual statements about a civilization. What, then, are indications of tomorrow's man, as judged by two trend-setting buildings which influence the lives of Arizonans in this, an era when the pyramids rise again?

Tempe, site of Arizona State University, boasts of a beautiful new Municipal Building unlike any other government office in the country. Designed by architects Michael and Kemper Goodwin and built by Sundt Construction Co. in 1970, the four-story building is an upside-down, glass-and-stone pyramid. Its capstone is sunk into the center of an underground complex of administrative offices. Roses, vines, and pine trees cascade down little sculptured hillocks, giving an aura of a resurrected Hanging Garden of Babylon.

Visitors who enter the building often exclaim, "It's so peaceful." On the top floor, which is actually the base, the mayor, city council, city attorney, and city clerk all work in uncluttered togetherness. The men at the top are performing their duties from the traditional bottom of the pyramid! Beyond their geographic confines, the southwestern states of the United States tend to have a long-range impact. They often provide leadership in manners and trends, true to the pioneer spirit that built this region. We can, therefore, assume that today's southwestern pyramid studies will be tomorrow's nationwide fascination, involvement, and experimentation.

Pyramids, Magnetism, and Gravity

by Alexander Ross

Eric McLuhan, who has created a plexiglass pyramid in his home in London, Ontario, is the subject of this contribution by Canadian writer Alexander Ross. As the author notes, Eric, now in his early thirties, is "very definitely a chip off the old block"—that being his father, Dr. Marshall McLuhan, whose daring sociopsychological concepts (including "The Medium Is the Message" and we're all part of a "Global Village," because of rapid communications) were popular concepts during the 1960's. But quite aside from his parental heritage, Eric McLuhan is an original thinker and experimenter—as his tests with pyramid power indicate.

Sitting on a table in Eric McLuhan's living room in London, Ontario, is a pyramid made of clear plexiglass, about eighteen inches high. Inside, on a little stand in the middle, he's placed a small hunk of hamburger, about the size of a sugar cube, and a small pellet of Cheddar cheese. Down in one corner of the pyramid's interior, two similar hunks of cheese and hamburger are sitting on the pyramid's base. They've been sitting there for three months now, and you can see a pronounced difference between the food on the stand and the food on the base.

"The meat on the stand—at the focal point of the pyramid's interior—is quite dry," says McLuhan, "and it looks a little frosty, as though it were glazed a tiny bit. You can easily distinguish between the lean and fat bits.

"But the hamburger in the corner? It's equally frosty-looking, but it's got sort of a purplish tinge. The cheese on the stand looks fresh. The food down in the corner is obviously not fit to eat."

McLuhan, the thirty-one-year-old son of the famous University of Toronto media philosopher, firmly believes that the pyramid in his living room has astonishing powers. By virtue of its shape alone, the angles of the plexiglass model are identical to those of the Great Pyramid in Egypt—he believes it can dehydrate meat, arrest bacterial growth, and, yes, sharpen razor blades.

"You simply take a dull blue-steel razor blade," says McLuhan; "for some reason, stainless steel doesn't seem to work too well. You put it on a platform inside the pyramid, one-third of the way from the bottom, with the edges of the blade lined up on a north-south axis. After about two weeks, it should be sharp enough to shave with again. If it is, take it out and shave with it, then drop it back in again. In two days at the most, it'll be ready to use again. From there on, just keep shaving with it, and leave it in the pyramid overnight. Some people get hundreds of shaves that way."

Eric McLuhan is very definitely a chip off the old block. Some sons react against famous fathers by being as unlike them as possible. Eric McLuhan is uncannily *like* his father, the author of that famous, and typically ambiguous slogan, The Medium Is the Message. Father and son are both brilliant, maddening eclectics. Both devour books as though they were popcorn. Both display an intellectual self-assurance that you find either awesome or irritating. Both have the sensibilities of poets and the jargon of scientists. Both display a tendency to confuse exciting possibilities with present realities. Both father and son can excite you with a concept one moment, and the next make you suspect you're the victim of a massive put-on. *A pyramid that sharpens razor blades?* What *is* this, anyway?

Implausible as it may seem, there is a lot of empirical evidence which indicates that a pyramid of the proper dimensions, perhaps because it amplifies or refracts certain forms of energy in ways we don't understand, will indeed perform the way Eric McLuhan says it does. Lots of people have tried it, and it seems to work.

John Rode, a Toronto disc jockey who runs an occult bookshop as a sideline, has been experimenting with pyramids for months, and is convinced they work. "We've been working with large ones, two-and-a-half feet tall," he says. "We're not sure what forces the pyramid amplifies, but whatever

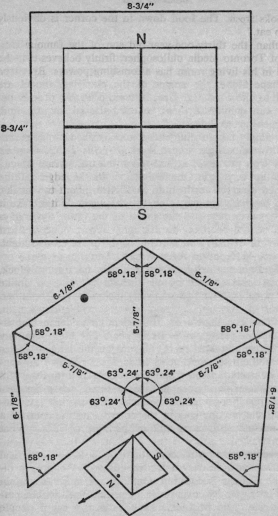

The two sketches, above, are working drawings used by Eric McLuhan in constructing his pyramids. The top drawing indicates the base, north-to-south, with measurements of the four sides given in inches. The bottom drawing shows the cut-out in inches and degrees, with a miniature of the completed pyramid reproduced, in outline, below.

they are, they do the job. They do indeed sharpen blue-steel razor blades, although we haven't had much luck with stainless steel. Also, I've used the pyramid to sharpen a steel knife, and we've dehydrated hundreds of eggs, and about ten pounds of porterhouse steak. It takes about twenty-three days to halt the decaying process in meat. You leave it under the pyramid and it doesn't go bad. Instead, it turns a little brown and eventually dries up. We've fried the steaks and eaten them, and they're delicious."

According to Lynn Schroeder and Sheila Ostrander, two Toronto-based writers whose book, *Psychic Discoveries Behind the Iron Curtain,* is a best-seller, the razor blade effect is common knowledge in Czechoslovakia, where people routinely preserve their blades in little cardboard pyramids that they keep in their bathrooms. One Czech pyramidologist, Karel Drbal, has even patented the shape of the Great Pyramid of Cheops, and cardboard models are now produced under license in the U.S. (You can buy one for $3 from Evering Associates, 43 Eglinton Avenue East, Toronto, or make one yourself; for a six-inch-high pyramid, the base must be nine and three-eighths inches on all four sides, and each sloping face must be eight and seven-eights inches long, or multiples of these.)

Unfortunately, there's no firm scientific evidence that the pyramid effect really exists. Researchers like McLuhan, who are experimenting with them, tend to be the kind of people who *want* them to work. And when McLuhan had an engineering consultant photograph a razor blade through a 100-pound microscope before and after three weeks inside a pyramid, no changes could be detected visually. "The test wasn't conclusive one way or the other," says the consultant, who wants to keep his name out of the mushrooming pyramid controversy. "All I know is that on that one test, we weren't able to replicate the results McLuhan obtained."

McLuhan now teaches a course in creative electronics at Fanshawe College in London, Ontario, where several of the students and faculty, experts in acoustics, are working off-hours on the problem. McLuhan believes that the pyramid's shape, in some way we don't understand, can manipulate the forces of magnetism and, yes, perhaps even gravity. McLuhan is suspicious of the prevailing notion that the pyramids were simply grandiose mausoleums, or what the ancient historian Pliny called an "idle and foolish exhibition of royal wealth."

"They're not just glorified tombstones," says McLuhan, "because many of them show no evidence of burial." Instead, from a study of the pyramids' changing shapes through several centuries, he believes that "the Egyptians were going through a number of development prototypes. The pyramids were the stone-age equivalent of the transistor and the semiconductor."

McLuhan got this insight last year, while teaching at the University of Wisconsin. He chanced on a picture of the famous Bent Pyramid at Dashur, and gasped: "Hey, that's a two-frequency octahedron"—a mathematically perfect shape studied by an old family friend named Buckminster Fuller. Floor plans of other pyramids astonished a friend of his, an acoustical engineer, who saw them. "It blew his mind," says McLuhan. "The plan looked exactly like a speaker system."

Were the pyramids some kind of stone prism used for channeling and redirecting some form of energy? Although the notion is, at the very least, pretty speculative, that's what McLuhan has been playing with for the past year. First, by building models in his garage in Wisconsin, he satisfied himself that they really do work. Then, he brainstormed the problem with a number of colleagues in various disciplines—physics, crystallography, acoustics, archaeology, ancient history—swarming up on the problem from all sides at once.

Eric McLuhan, like his father, is a passionate generalist. The reason pyramids have remained an enigma," he says, "is the separation between the disciplines. If an archaeologist knows nothing about electronics, he's not likely to see that the pyramids were *tools*—sophisticated pieces of technology."

Well, if they are tools, how do they work, and what did they do for the Egyptians? McLuhan has a lot of speculative comment on that point, untested but fascinating. The razor blade and dehydration effects may happen, he suspects, as a consequence of a "coherent magnetic field" inside the pyramid. It's known, for instance, that oxygen atoms behave differently inside different magnetic fields; they can affect the way they combine with, or disassociate from, atoms of other elements. A similar resonant juggling of molecular structure, only this time with iron compounds, would perhaps account for the "sharpening" or reconstitution of razor blade edges.

Other investigators have speculated that the pyramid's shape is similar to that of the structure of various crystalline compounds, including the metal edge of a razor blade, and that the twin shapes somehow set up sympathetic vibrations with each other. But these are just guesses and, to my knowledge, they've never been subjected to rigorous scientific testing.

McLuhan asked a friend at Northern Electric's laboratories in Ottawa, for instance, to attempt to grow semiconductor crystals inside a pyramid. Semiconductors, one of the basic building-blocks of miniaturized electronics, are sensitive to all kinds of radiation. McLuhan hoped that a semiconductor grown in a magnetically pure environment might turn out to be wondrously efficient. Unfortunately, nothing's been done about the idea. The apparatus for growing semiconductors looks like a cross between a die stamping machine and an electron microscope, and Northern Electric's scientists haven't got the time, money, or inclination to build a garage-size pyramid to check it out.

Still, there's a seductive amount of evidence to suggest that something weird happens at the focal point inside a pyramid. Schroeder and Ostrander, in their book, report that in 1968, scientists at Egypt's Ein Sham University used computers and X-ray machines to record and analyze the pattern of cosmic rays reaching the interior of the Chephren Pyramid near Cairo. They were looking for hidden chambers inside the pyramid, but the results baffled them. The cosmic ray patterns inside the pyramid varied sharply from day to day. "This is scientifically impossible," the project's director, Dr. Amr Gohed, told *The Times* of London. Whatever was happening inside the pyramid, he said, "defies all the known laws of science and electronics."

Magnetism one can begin to accept. But gravity? Yes, McLuhan suspects the two forces are related, and that the pyramids manipulated both. "How else did they get those huge stones across the desert?" he asks. "The conventional explanation is that they used rollers. But have you ever tried to pull a car out of the sand? It's almost impossible." He postulates some technology, unknown to us, which could deprive an object of some of its gravitational pull, but not its mass. That way, blocks could simply be floated across the desert. Fanciful, but there are other considerations—such as the existence of one unfinished pyramid which still has ramps in place, and Egyptian paintings from a later period showing men hauling a huge stone in a sledge.

The mystery of the pyramids has fascinated scientists and philosophers for centuries. It has also intrigued a great many plain nuts. There are many cults, from the Rosicrucians to the Masonic order which deal heavily in fanciful pyramid lore. McLuhan may very well be the latest, and by far the most articulate, in a long and unscientific line of pyramid freaks.

But suppose he's on to something? Twenty years ago, his father's poetic insights about how the communications media affect our sensory balance, and thus the way a society perceives the world, were dismissed as fanciful and unscientific. Well, yes, they are; but there are very few educators or communicators today who don't acknowledge some debt to Marshall McLuhan.

Is it wholly inconceivable that the ancient Egyptians, a culture far older than ours, knew some things about technology that we don't know, but are beginning to rediscover?

An Oraccu Is Not
a Pyramid—Or Is It?

by Serge V. King

Dr. King is a widely traveled management specialist and linguist of great versatility. While program director in West Africa for Catholic Relief Services (1964–1971), he was engaged in social services in Togo, Dahomey, Senegal, Gambia, Mauritania, and Mali. In addition to several Western languages, Serge King learned to speak the African language of Wolof and became acquainted with Hassania, a Berber-Arab dialect. Dr. King is now engaged in research in parapsychology and paraphysics; he directs Huna International Life Systems Research in Los Angeles, California. His current language study is Polynesian.

Experiments with a baffling source of energy brought about the downfall of Wilhelm Reich, one of Sigmund Freud's brightest pupils. Though he was once thought to be the protégé on whom the mantle of Freudian philosophy and prestige would descend, Reich died in prison after being convicted of contempt of court because he refused to defend the existence of what he considered a natural phenomenon. Today he is still regarded as one of the most controversial scientists of this century. He insisted that the energy force he was working with was not a new nor unknown energy. He called it "orgone" energy and said it had a lengthy history. Reich wrote about it, recorded his experiments, and reported his theories and observations. His once popular books were banned for a time by judicial process of the United States government. Reich could not define nor prove his observations scientifically enough to satisfy the established practitioners in his field, who thought him too far out.

148

But surprising as it seems, our brainiest scientists still do not know what light, electricity, magnetism, radio waves, X-rays, gamma rays and other baffling observable sources of energy really are. They have measured, quantified, qualified, and used these energies. But any honest scientist must admit that understanding their true nature is still largely speculative. Definitions usually fall into analogies, and these in turn lead us into a semantic quagmire that serves only to add to the confusion.

Yet, daily we take these strange forces for granted. They comfort us. Any challenge to this established comfort is met as a threat. Some ignore it, others attack it, the courageous investigate it. Small wonder that we find it difficult to deal with energy forces we cannot easily describe.

For many millennia, a disturbing energy force was rather clumsily described as originating in the body. Not everyone could control it, so it was often suspiciously regarded as a disturbance. It was often classified as a subjective experience, hence a delusion. This is the force that intrigued Reich.

In China, this energy was called *ch'i*, in India *prana*, in Polynesia *mana*, and in Europe *vital force*. Now, the most acceptable term is *psychotronic energy*. The Russians are said to be about twenty years ahead of the U.S. in the study and application of this energy force.

The first modern investigation of this psychotronic energy was carried out by Franz Anton Mesmer about 200 years ago. His studies gave us the term *mesmerism*, often erroneously equated only with hypnotism. Mesmer called the energy he discovered *animal magnetism* because he thought magnets were its source, and believed it shared many, but not all, properties of conventional magnetism. Hypnotism was only a by-product of Mesmer's work, though of tremendous importance in its own right. Some of the observable qualities of animal magnetism are polarity, reflectivity, the ability to penetrate all materials, and the capability of being accumulated, stored, and transported in both animate and inanimate objects.

Nearly fifty years after Mesmer, Baron Charles von Reichenbach undertook some extensive studies of animal magnetism, which he renamed *odic force*, or simply *od*. Reichenbach noted all the qualities discovered by Mesmer, plus many more. He thought od was automatically generated by such diverse substances as crystals, magnets, electric motors, and the human body. Visually, he reported, the force could be seen as a bluish or reddish light, depending on polarity. The blue gave off a sensation of coolness; red, heat.

Unfortunately, Reichenbach depended on human sensitivity as a measuring device. His work was disparaged and ignored.

In this century, psychotronic energy was rediscovered by the ill-fated Wilhelm Reich. He called it "orgone." Reich claimed he produced orgone under laboratory conditions and carried out thousands of controlled tests on it. He claimed to be able to measure it thermically, electrostatically, and by means of a Geiger counter. He found it could be generated by specially constructed boxes, tubes, and other devices, as well as in the human body. Additional orgone qualities reported by Reich were a dehydration effect, a drawing effect, but a deadly effect when the energy was brought into contact with radioactive materials. He is also said to have developed it as a power source to run a motor. It is interesting to note that the Soviet government ordered all of the written works of Reich before they were banned by the U.S. government in the late 1950's. Only a few of Reich's books are still available.

The most recently reported rediscovery of psychotronic energy was made by Czechoslovakian scientists. The fascinating details are found in the book, *Psychic Discoveries Behind the Iron Curtain*. Briefly, the major Czech addition to the knowledge is that pyramidal-shaped objects acted as generators of the energy by means of their shape alone. They call this psychotronic energy now beginning to interest U.S. scientists.

Every discoverer of this energy has stressed its considerable power to heal or stimulate healing of the human body.

My own investigation of this energy began accidentally. I read about the Czech experiments with pyramids and was intrigued. But like most people, I merely stored the information in my memory file of curious facts. Then one day I happened to find one of Wilhelm Reich's books. It was easy to correlate some of Reich's theories with some of my own. These are the synthesized observations:

1. Pyramids appear to have a strange power to dehydrate organic material.

2. Reich's orgone dehydration affected human subjects.

3. Pyramids can be observed to have the power to sharpen razor blades.

4. Plastic is apparently capable of absorbing orgone energy.

5. A combination of metal and nonmetalic substances appears to enhance the generation of orgone energy.

6. A razor blade that I habitually kept in its razor and stored in a small plastic box remained sharp for an unusually long period of time. I determined to learn whether I had in-

advertently been using orgone energy, and whether that was the same as pyramid energy.

I began keeping a record of the number of shaves I obtained. The blade was stored between shaves as mentioned. The blade was a Gillette Platinum Plus. After 200 smooth shaves, for the most part on consecutive days, I decided more serious experimentation was in order. I could find no indication that Reich had ever used what he called an orgone accumulator (*oraccu*, for short) for sharpening anything.

To carry out my experiment, I used an inexpensive Gillette Blue Blade, because I felt the sharpening effect, if any, would be more noticeable. An identical blade, used as a control and simply left on the counter between shaves, gave only seven shaves before it was too dull to use.

The test blade was kept in an all-metal razor and stored in a 2 x 4 x 1-inch plastic box. Not until the 22nd shave did it become even slightly rough. Inexplicably, it was smooth the next day and remained so until the 29th shave, when it again became rough. It stayed fairly rough for the next four shaves. Then I got another idea.

Up to now, I had not placed the box or the blade in any special direction, but I remembered that orientation was a very important factor in the pyramids. I faced the short ends of the box in a north-south direction. The blade, still in the razor, was at one end of the box, perpendicular to the storage counter. The short ends of the blade faced east-west. The next three shaves were smooth. There then began a period in which the blade would be smooth one day and rough the next. So I reoriented the blade with its edges facing east and west. The next six shaves were all very smooth.

There was no doubt that the orientation to magnetic North was having an observable effect, but now I wondered whether the razor itself was a factor. I removed the blade from the razor and replaced it in the box, following the previous alignment. The very next shave was rough. I concluded the metal razor was interacting with the plastic box to produce the sharpening effect. As soon as I reintroduced the razor into the picture, the blade sharpened up again. It was time to run another check on the orientation. I changed the orientation of the box by 90 degrees, but left the blade in the same position. To my surprise it remained sharp, showing that the orientation of the object was more important than the orientation of the box.

Well, my crazy little box and razor setup was doing things it had no right to do. Seventy-two shaves with a Gillette Blue

Blade? A rough blade getting sharp overnight? I thought there was some kind of energy at work. Maybe Reich wasn't such a nut after all.

I decided to give Reich's ideas a full work-out by converting my plastic box to a full-fledged oraccu. The principle of an oraccu is based on the theory that nonmetallic materials such as paper, plastic, wood, and stone absorb orgone energy from the atmosphere and hold it, while metals absorb it and instantly release it. How long that takes I do not know. Therefore, if a sheet of metal is placed next to a sheet of nonmetal, the latter will absorb some orgone. The metal will absorb a part and then expel it into the nearest free air space. It sounds similar to the action of a Voltaic battery, except that no electrolyte is involved and no measurable electric current is present.

The conversion was simple. I lined the box with aluminum foil. In the center, resting on a quarter-inch-high rubber washer, I placed the razor blade. The next four shaves were excellent. I moved both the box and the blade out of their north-south alignment, and after three more shaves it was too rough to use. In none of Reich's extant writings had I noticed anything about an orientation effect, but it was certainly operating here. By realigning the blade, I got 12 more shaves ranging from fair to quite smooth. After that, it began to take two days for the blade to sharpen instead of one. This was at the end of 104 shaves.

I was beginning to feel sorry for the poor overworked blade, but I had to try something else. According to Reich, the intensity or strength of orgone can be increased by increasing the number of nonmetal and metal layers in an oraccu. Each layer is called a *fold* in the language of Orgonomy.

For the next test, I made a three-fold oraccu out of styrofoam and aluminum foil. After twenty-four hours my rough blade was smooth again, and it stayed smooth as long as I replaced it in the new oraccu after each shave. It wasn't as smooth as a brand-new one, so I tried leaving it in the oraccu for a whole week to see if that would improve it, but I detected no difference between a week and twenty-four hours. Since the onefold oraccu no longer had any (or very little) effect on the blade, I had to conclude that I was dealing with an actual increase in the energy.

It is hard to put my excitement on paper. A razor blade isn't supposed to suddenly get sharp again after being too dull to use. It is true that the edge of a razor blade is what is known technically as a *live* crystal formation. So, if it's left by itself for a long enough period it will automatically regain some of its original sharpness. But it isn't supposed to do so overnight, not by just leaving it in a box, regardless of what the box is made of. It isn't supposed to automatically sharpen because, until now, we haven't known of any logical explanation for it to. I still don't know why it does; I only know that it works. How many of us know why our television sets and car engines work? Who knows why gravity works? We have to settle for making use of all the odd energies around by properly utilizing their specific properties. A razor blade may not seem important, but it is the implication of having been instrumental in causing certain repeatable, observable effects on the blade by means of a heretofore unrecognized energy that must make everyone take note.

I carried on numerous other experiments which served to prove a relation between the energy of the oraccu and that of the pyramid forms. For instance, both are equally good at dehydrating meat, fruits, and vegetables, but as yet I have not worked out a relationship between the comparative sizes of each that are required to do the same job. A pyramid which is layered like an oraccu seems to work better than a plain one.

One thing that bothered me about the accounts of pyramid research was the flat statement that the object to be acted upon had to be placed one-third of the way up from the base to the apex. I decided to test this for myself by using a six-inch-high pyramid of cardboard and pieces of apple. One piece of apple was kept outside the pyramid as a control. From my diary, here are my conclusions:

1. If there is an energy concentration at the apex of the pyramid, it is either of such a nature as not to have a dehydration effect, or it is too weak.

2. There is no concentration of dehydrating energy at the base of the pyramid.

3. The focal point for dehydrating energy in a pyramid is one half to one third of the distance from the base to the apex, in the center of the pyramid.

It will be noticed that I am careful to specify "dehydrating energy." For all I know, there may be other effects at different levels. It has been reported that there is an energy beam stretching upward from the apex of pyramids, but it doesn't effect dehydration.

An experiment with water showed a definite correlation between pyramids and oraccus. Pyramids are said to purify water, so I placed a glass of plain tap water under a six-inch pyramid overnight, making sure the water level reached up to the midway point. I left an identical glass of water standing on a table in the same room. The next morning, I used my family as guinea pigs and had them taste the two glasses of water without telling them which was which. Four out of four said there was a distinct difference in taste, and three out of four preferred the water that was under the pyramid. As for myself, admitting that I knew which was which, the water that had been under the pyramid tasted purer, almost sweet, far better than the water straight from the tap. Exactly what had happened to it I would not venture to say without a laboratory analysis. I did note that there were more bubbles present in the pyramid water than in the water I left out. Identical experiments were carried out with water left overnight in oraccus, with identical results.

Without raising too many eyebrows, all the previous experiments can be carried out by anyone. The results are easily demonstrable. The next experiments will seem pretty far out to most people. But since we don't really know the exact nature of the energy we are dealing with, we have to set aside a lot of preconceptions. The results are likely to be quite subjective. We are constantly bombarded with extrasensory inputs which we do not normally perceive because we have never developed the talent for it. Take wine-tasting, for example. An expert wine-taster can tell from a single sip of wine the geographical origin of the grape, the type of soil it was grown in, who produced it, whether or not it was blended, the year it was bottled, and whether or not it has any future in the bottle. Using other specially developed senses, an expert mechanic can analyze an engine by its sound.

I can feel with my hands the energy coming out of the top of a pyramid and the concentration in an oraccu. It feels cool, like the odic force described by Reichenbach. This is not something I was born with. I consciously developed it, as I might any other sense. Now, because I could feel the energy from the pyramid as a cool sort of breeze, I thought there might be something to the cool breeze effect reported by Reichenbach in his work with magnets. Accordingly, I obtained a small but fairly powerful magnet and ran it along my palm, as Reichenbach recommended. Sure enough, I felt a cool, tingling sensation. Taking advantage of my family again, I tried the magnet out without telling them what to expect. My children, aged ten, seven, and six, all reported the same effect I had felt, but my wife felt nothing at all. I have not had time to follow this up, but the sensation from the pyramid and the magnet is the same. I think it demonstrates a connection. Some pyramid experimenters claim that placing a magnet inside a pyramid increases the energy.

I obtained a plastic tube about forty inches long and two inches in diameter to test Reich's theory that tubes draw orgone from the atmosphere because of their shape. I was amazed to feel the same sort of cool breeze effect when passing a hand over one end of the tube. To test this further, I had my wife hold the tube while I closed my eyes and turned in a circle to disorient myself, and then I attempted to find the location by feel alone. My hand stopped right over it five times out of five, an easy feat because I could feel the breeze.

Curious to see what effect the energy might have on the mind, I meditated with an open-base, six-inch pyramid on my head. I did this late at night, of course, in order to avoid some friendly family jeering. The effects were remarkable. At first, the pyramid seemed to be rolling around on my head and I had to touch it to make sure it wasn't really moving. A few moments later, it seemed to grow tighter until it felt like a close-fitting cap. After that, my mind's eye was swamped with a swift series of dreamlike sequences of great clarity, but no comprehensible meaning. Unrecognizable characters walked about and seemed to be talking in a normal setting. In seconds, the scene changed. It was much like being shown a succession of motion picture film clips stuck together without rhyme or reason.

Thousands of experiments must be tried before we can get a clear picture of the effects of this "new" energy and find ways to apply it for the good of humanity.

For those brave souls with a healthy spirit of adventure, here are the measurements for building a six-inch pyramid of your own:

Using cardboard, plastic, or any nonmetallic material, cut four triangles whose sides are 8 and 7/8 inches, and whose base is 9 and 3/8 inches, and tape or glue them together. *Voilà!* That's it. One side of the pyramid has to face north. The further off alignment, the less effective it is.

As for the oraccu, the description given above should suffice to make one in any size you want. Reich warned about the danger of using anything stronger than a threefold oraccu for home use, though, so proceed cautiously.

Pyramids Around the World

by Warren Smith

The U.S. Army Air Force pilot flying over the China-India "Hump" in World War Two saw a "gigantic white pyramid" within a level valley. To him, it looked "like something out of a fairy tale," shimmering white and with a crystal-like capstone. Other pyramids, some as elusive as this one and others well-known structures, can be found elsewhere in Asia, as well as in Central and South America. Mr. Smith, author of many books on psychic phenomena and mysterious events, examines the many hypotheses connected with ancient pyramids, including their possible links to astronomy, legendary Atlantis, and secret knowledge of past civilizations.

The greatest wonder of the world may be hidden in a remote Himalayan mountain valley. A gigantic pyramid, encased in shimmering white stone and topped with a dazzling jeweled capstone, has been a legend in Asia for centuries. The precise location of this enigmatic marvel is unknown. However, U.S. airmen reported flying over similar structures during WW II.

"I know the legend about the white pyramid is true. I've seen it with my own eyes," reported James Gaussman, a WW II pilot from New Orleans, La. "The men who flew cargo over 'The Hump' saw some pretty strange things below them. There were sightings of lost cities, strange buildings in the wilderness, and old ruins in lost valleys. Pyramids were just part of the whole mystery of the Himalayan Mountains."

James Gaussman flew perilous "dead man's alley" in a cargo plane during WW II. This was across the brutal "Hump," a 500-mile stretch of towering, uncharted mountains between India and China. The hazardous aerial operation supplied Nationalist Chinese armies with guns and vital supplies after the Japanese occupied the entire coastline closing all seafronts. The transport planes faced dangerous natural hazards unlike anything else in the world. Asian monsoons, Tibetan ice storms, and thick banks of clouds made each flight a high-risk venture.

"Some of those trips were absolute nightmares," Gaussman recalls. "Sometimes we'd get too high above the mountains and our wings would ice up. If we flew between the mountains, we encountered fog and clouds. Flying a creaky plane, with a load of shifting crates, between snow-covered mountains is hard on the nerves. If visibility was near zero, it was possible to miss seeing the mountain and more than one plane crashed into a peak."

In early 1942, Gaussman was on a mission when his plane developed engine trouble.

"The engine started cutting out," he recalled. "I dropped to a lower altitude figuring the gas lines were freezing up. The other planes went on. The rule out there was that anyone in trouble was on his own. We dropped low and started zigzagging through the mountains until the engines cleared up."

Gaussman was following a flight path that would bring him back to his base in Assam, India. "I banked to avoid a mountain and we came out over a level valley," he related. "Directly below was a gigantic white pyramid. It looked like something out of a fairy tale. It was encased in shimmering white. This could have been metal, or some sort of stone. It was pure white on all sides. The remarkable thing was the capstone, a huge piece of jewel-like material that could have been crystal."

Gaussman made three passes over the pyramid.

"There was no way we could have landed, although we wanted to," he stated. "We were struck by the immensity of the thing."

Flying in and out of the mountains, Gaussman picked up the Brahmaputra River. He landed safely at the airfield in Assam. "We made a report on the white pyramid to the intelligence officer at the base," he continued. "He said later that he'd done nothing about it. The war took priority and, after a few weeks, I transferred out. I always wanted to hunt down that pyramid, maybe get an expedition and go back into the mountains. That takes time, money, and effort and I have to earn a living."

Gaussman believes the pyramid will be discovered.

"I don't know how soon it will be," he said, "because those Himalayan Mountains are still unmapped. The discovery will electrify the world when it does come. There was nothing around it—just a big pyramid sitting out in the middle of this valley. I figure it was extremely old. Who built it? Why was it built? What's on the inside? I suppose I'll never know the answers to those questions."

Gaussman's story of Asia's white pyramid is intriguing. Did he really see it, or was it a figment of a vivid imagination? He admits there is no physical evidence to verify his report. However, students of pyramids point out that these strange, tetrahedron-shaped structures have been found throughout the world. Explorers, soldiers of fortune, scientists, and treasure hunters have returned from uncharted regions of our globe with reports of lost pyramids.

"What may appear to be a natural hill from an aerial view may be a pyramid," reported Dr. Gunther Rosenberg, founder and former president of the European Occult Research Association. "Pyramids are often found covered with natural growth. This is often the case in Central and South America."

It would seem that ancient humans constructed a mysterious network of pyramids throughout the world. Or did they?

If they did, we don't know their reasons for building these remarkable stone monuments.

We do not know how they were built.

A furious scientific debate rages over the methods supposedly used by ancient craftsmen to construct these enormous structures. "Can we believe the historians?" asked Dr. Gunther Rosenberg. "Without a knowledge of technology, without modern equipment, and without advanced mathematics, we're asked to believe that a simple, primitive group of people built the pyramids. This is like attributing the huge skyscrapers in America to the work of schoolchildren!"

Dr. Rosenberg believes more knowledge concerning man's origin will be developed when the mystery of the pyramids is solved.

"At least part, perhaps all, of the answer may be linked to the pyramids," he declared. "I attach no special occult significance to the pyramids. They are simply there and should be studied by a panel of open-minded scientists. As yet, science has not produced a satisfactory explanation for the pyramids."

Scholars and scientists have debated the meaning of the Great Pyramid for centuries. The Cheops Pyramid is located on the barren Gizeh plateau near Cairo, the largest known *stone* pyramid in the world. With casing stones intact, scientists estimate the structure soared 485 feet into the hot desert air.

The Great Pyramid contains six and a half million tons of stones, each weighing from three to sixty tons. The base covers thirteen acres. Construction experts have estimated the cost of building the pyramid today would be around $4.5 billion.

"It is the pinnacle of human achievement in ancient times," reported Dr. Rosenberg.

Some occultists claim the Great Pyramid is a durable record of ancient science. Madame Blavatsky, founder of Theosophy, author of *The Secret Doctrine,* and one of the most controversial occult leaders in the 1800's, said the Great Pyramid was an ageless record of the principles of mathematics, scientific data, and mystical truths.

Madame Blavatsky also felt that secret chambers inside the Great Pyramid were used by mystical societies for the initiation of members. "The idea of a group of Masters, men who guarded secret knowledge, has long been associated with the pyramids," admitted Dr. Rosenberg. "On the other hand, many religious people have attempted to link biblical prophesy with the measurements of the pyramids."

In Arabian folklore, the pyramids are connected with the Great Flood of the Bible. A manuscript preserved in the Bodleian Library, at Oxford University, England, by Arab historian Abou Balkhi says:

". . . The wise men, previous to the flood, foreseeing an impending judgment from heaven, either by submersion or fire, which would destroy every created thing, built upon the tops of the mountains in Upper Egypt many pyramids of stone, in order to have some refuge from the approaching calamity. Two of these buildings exceeded the rest in height, being 400 cubits high and as many broad and as many long. They were built with large blocks of marble, and they were so well put together that the joints were scarcely perceptible. Upon the interior of the building every charm and wonder of physics was inscribed."

There are certainly unusual measurements built into the Great Pyramid.

• Measurements multiplied to the tenth power total 91,840,000 miles, the approximate distance of the Earth from the Sun. Also, galleys and passageways contain a variety of complex mathematical relationships.

• The Great Pyramid was built on a precise north-south axis (it has shifted slightly to the west). The builders understood both advanced mathematics and global geography. Historians say ancient Egyptians had no knowledge of *pi,* yet this mathematical measurement is used in the pyramids.

• Ancient Egyptians had scientific knowledge of the heavens, the course of the stars, and the movement of heavenly bodies. Some scholars believe the Great Pyramid also served as an ancient astronomical observatory.

Lost somewhere in U.S. Army files is an aerial photograph of the mysterious Shensi pyramid in China. Taken in 1947 from a low-flying army transport, the photograph shows the giant structure, which lies several days travel west of the ancient Chinese capital of Sian-fu, a walled city that is older than Peking.

In 1912, Fred Meyer Schroeder and his partner, Oscar Maman, were trading guns and supplies to Chinese warlords. "We heard about the city when we were in Sian-fu," Schroeder told newsmen years later. "A Buddhist priest said the pyramid was in a westerly direction from the city. We rode for two days along the old caravan road that runs all the way from the Mediterranean Sea into Peking. We inquired along the way, and, in one small village, we discovered the pyramid was about a day's ride north."

Late the next afternoon, Schroeder and his partner sighted the pyramid in the distance. "It was about 1,000 feet high 1,500 feet at the base," Schroeder said. "This would make it larger than the Great Pyramid in Egypt." The four sides of the pyramid were coordinated to the compass points. Later, while visiting a retreat, Schroeder was told that ancient records revealed the Shensi pyramid was at least 6,000 years old.

Frank Stephens, a soldier of fortune, also heard about the Shensi pyramid when he was wandering through the Orient in the 1930's. "The Shensi pyramid is probably the largest man-made structure on Earth," he said. "Schroeder and Maman said it was 1,000 feet high; I'd judge it to be at least 1,200 feet in height. Each side of the pyramid had been painted a different color, green to the east, red to the south, black to the west, and white for the north. The pyramid had a flat, uncapped top with traces of yellow paint."

Stephens found what may have been casing stones at the base of the Shensi structure. "They were hewn from ordinary field stone," he stated. "The pyramid itself appeared to be constructed from pounded earth. This is an old Chinese method of building whereby lime and clay are mixed together. It hardens like cement into an adobe-like material. Although the pyramid is well-constructed, there is considerable decay. Rock and debris have started coming out of the interior, forming sizable ridges and gullies on the outside walls."

Stephens reported there were seven flat-topped pyramids in remote areas of Shensi Province. "A mile beyond the big fellow is a smaller, flat-topped pyramid that soars about 500 feet into the air," he said. "There was another structure another mile beyond the second one. Several miles away, four more smaller pyramids were aligned in a true north-south pattern."

Intrigued by the pyramids, Stephens inquired about their origin. The natives in that region were unable to provide any information.

"The local peasants didn't know who built them," said Stephens. "All they know is that the pyramids have been here as long as anyone can remember. The U.S. Army photograph was released in 1947 and it was published in the newspapers. It was like reliving those days when I was wandering through China. I've always wondered what group of people built them. I wonder about their reasons for building them out in the backwoods of Shensi."

Once the Bamboo Curtain is removed, scientists may be able to inspect the Shensi pyramids. "In 1937 Mao Tse-tung ended his Long March in Yenan, in north Shensi province," said Stephens. "The Chinese Communists controlled that region for ten years. Then (in 1949), they took over all of China. Since then, we've had a news blackout on matters inside China. Perhaps an expedition can go into Shensi in a few years and explore these pyramids."

Whoever built the Shensi pyramids may have gone farther into Central Asia and carved the little-known Bamian statues. These statues have been there for countless centuries, defying natural catastrophes and man's instincts for destruction. In her *Secret Doctrine*, Madame Blavatsky writes:

"Bamian is a small, miserable, half-ruined town in Central Asia, halfway between Cabul and Balkh, at the foot of the Koh-i-baba, a huge mountain of the Paropanisian, or Hindukush, chain, some 8,500 feet above sea level. In days of old, Bamian was a portion of the ancient city of Djooljool, ruined and destroyed to the last stone by Genghis-Kahn in the 13th Century.

". . . The whole valley is hemmed in by colossal rocks, which are full of partially natural and partially artificial caves and grottoes, once the dwelling place of Buddhist monks . . . In front of these caves five enormous statues—of what is regarded as Buddha—have been discovered or rather rediscovered in our century, for the famous Chinese traveler Hiouen Thsang speaks of having seen them when he visited Bamian in the 7th Century."

Madame Blavatsky compared the Bamian statues to other monuments. "Thus, the largest of the Bamian statues is 173 feet high, or *70* feet higher than the Statue of Liberty now at New York," she wrote.

By comparison, it might be noted, the busts of the Presidents sculpted at Mt. Rushmore National Memorial in South Dakota, are sixty feet from chin to forehead.

Who placed the statues at Bamian? They may have been the same builders who constructed pyramids throughout ancient India. "The *puranas* is a holy book of the Hindu religion," reported Dr. Gunther Rosenberg. "These ancient texts tell of scores of pyramids throughout India, dating back to prehistory. These structures were apparently so old that they've crumbled to dust, been destroyed by vandals, or torn down to build ancient cities."

In our country, anthropologists have started to dig into the mysteries of a masssive pyramid at Cahokia Mounds State Park, Collinsville, Ill. This incredible earthen pyramid is located a few minutes' drive from downtown St. Louis, Mo. Measuring 100 feet high, 1,000 feet long, and 800 feet wide, the Cahokia pyramid has a base larger than the Great Pyramid in Egypt.

Experts have estimated that the builders required 250 years to move twenty-one million cubic feet of earth to the site. They used simple prehistoric flint tools and baskets. Although the Cahokia pyramid is the largest prehistoric structure in the U.S., it was totally ignored until the current excavations were started.

"We never thought much about it," is the way a Collinsville businessman explained the town's attitude. "It's always been there, and we used to play on it as kids. It was just a funny looking hill covered with brush and weeds."

The pyramid is a part of an enormous complex of ruins at Cahokia. Dr. Nelson Reed, anthropologist at Washington University in St. Louis, believes Cahokia was the site of "a lost Indian civilization, with sacrificial pits, sun gods, pyramids, a great wall, and human sacrifices." Dr. Reed has excavated many of the sites.

At the time of its maximum development, according to present knowledge, Cahokia was home for 250,000 Indians. This would make Cahokia the largest settlement inside our borders for hundreds of years!

The area was probably settled around 700 A.D. by Woodland Indians who hunted and fished there. Later generations planted corn in the fertile valley and launched an agricultural society. Somewhere along the way, they started trading with other tribes and extended their trading expeditions from the Rocky Mountains to the Eastern Seaboard. Still later, the Cahokia Indians set up additional colonies in far-flung areas 1,000 miles or more from their city. These colonies were located in Georgia, Mississippi, Kansas, Wisconsin, Arkansas, and Minnesota. Like the outposts on the borders of the Roman Empire, these colonies may have been used both for trading and "occupation" of the territory of other tribes. Archaeologsts claim the Cahokians reigned supreme for about 500 years.

What caused the city to fall? Anthropologists report that 100 years before Columbus sailed from Spain, Cahokia had started to decline in power and prestige. The climate may have changed; a drought would create immense problems for a chief ruling over a city of a quarter of a million people. Enormous herds of buffalo moved east about this time, perhaps destroying everything in their path. In 1700, when French explorers came downriver, Indians in the region claimed Cahokia had been destroyed by "the Great Spirit."

I believe the giant pyramid may have been responsible for Cahokia's downfall. To move twenty-one million cubic feet of dirt for the pyramid would require a good percentage of the males in the tribe. Plus, by using 10 or 20 percent of their strongest men to build the pyramid, the loss of manpower would weaken any settlement. War parties from other tribes, eager for plunder and captives from the largest Indian settle-

ment then in existence, may have eventually broken through
Cahokia's defenses and overrun the city.

Leaving southern Illinois, we find another interesting pyramid site near the tiny community of Williams, Mont. A
mysterious series of mini-pyramids, about three feet tall, are
located north of that community. The Montana Historical
Society has reported these are possibly markers for some
unknown band of sheepherders. S. D. Bufmeyer of Puyallup,
Wash., visited the site a few years ago and disagrees with
this explanation.

In a letter to *Fate* magazine, Bufmeyer discovered the
pyramids were constructed along a northwest-southwest line.
". . . It is clearly evident by following the course and direction of the line that the pyramids did not get there by
chance," he reported. "Further, from their appearance they
might be thousands of years old, possibly built by an ancient
system or school of science. I am positive that an archaeologist would find these pyramids interesting for research and
particularly in regard to the direction they take over the
rough sagebrush country."

Bufmeyer did not report on whether the Montana mini-
pyramids were constructed of stone or earth. As I have not
visited the site, I can provide no additional details. Dr. Gunther Rosenberg believes there may be many "lost" pyramids
throughout the world. "We may be talking about a time span
of several thousand years," he explained. "Earth changes, bad
weather, and natural growth will certainly change the appearance of a pyramid over the centuries."

Before we dismiss mini-pyramids in Montana's sagebrush
country, let's look at a pyramidal mound at Painted Rock
Reservoir near Gila Bend, Ariz. This mini-pyramid was dis-
covered in 1959 by University of Arizona archaeologists.
They theorized the flat-topped structure was used by ancient
Indians for religious ceremonies.

The Arizona pyramid has been dated at 900 to 1150 A.D.,
similar to the Cahokia pyramid. This mini-pyramid was enlarged several times like Cahokia, indicating the possible use
of a Mexican calendar by southwestern Indians. "It was the
custom to enlarge pyramids in Mexico every fifty-two years,"
explained an archaeologist. "Their calendars equated fifty-two
years to our century on a modern calendar."

Rumors of pyramids in Alaska were published in a letter
in *Fate* magazine in July, 1962. Mercedes B. Madders, of
Jackson, Mont., wrote:

"I have heard that an ancient village is located not far from Ketchikan, Alaska. I believe I am the only person alive who has heard of this place. It was discovered by an old prospector who, after falling off a clump of rocks and examining the place where he fell, discovered it was a *man-made pyramid* (italics added). The valley reportedly contains man-made canals on the hill said to be in ruins. I know the area in which the ruins are situated.

"I have visited a spot not too many miles from this alleged secret location where a homesteader, while plowing a small beach area for a garden patch, discovered all sorts of artifacts."

Rumors of lost pyramids amid old ruins can easily be dismissed as folklore. Sometimes, an adventurous person tracks down the stories and proves their truth. Michael Piessel, just out of college, did that when he made scores of startling discoveries in Mexico during the late 1950's.

Piessel was vacationing in Mexico when he became intrigued by the vacant space on the maps of Quintana Roo, which is along the Mexican east coast, north of British Honduras. Piessel noticed that there were towns along the coast, about a day's walking distance apart. He decided to walk down Quintana Roo, the most savage coastline in North America.

Not fully realizing the dangers of the jungles, Piessel took a bus from Mexico City, chartered a plane to ferry him to the island of Cozumel, then hitched a ride across the Gulf of Mexico in a fisherman's boat.

The fisherman dropped Piessel on a beach near an Indian family's hut, promising to return with supplies in a few days. A week later, Piessel realized he had been stranded on the desolate coast. The Indians explained it might be months before another boat arrived. They also revealed their concern about Piessel's appetite. "Food is scarce here," he was told. "You must leave."

Piessel had also learned that the towns on his map were nonexistent, mere figments of a mapmaker's dreams. He would have to rely on his luck to walk the 200 miles down the coast to the nearest town. He strapped on his sandals, picked up his knapsack, and walked into the dangerous jungles.

In the weeks that followed he encountered warlike Indians, bandits, machete-waving chicle workers, and natural jungle hazards. Piessel also discovered the coast was dotted with

Mayan ruins, *many containing pyramids.* He explored secret passageways, mapped lost towns, and plucked jade jewelry from one site. His adventure was recounted in *The Lost World of Quintana Roo.*

Besides Piessel's new pyramid discoveries, Mexico has other vast structures including the Pyramid of the Sun and Moon, outside Mexico City. The Pyramid of the Sun measures 761 by 721 feet, larger at the base than the Cheops Pyramid in Egypt. Both of these flat-topped pyramids are perfectly oriented between north and south.

"When Cortez explored Mexico he discovered pyramids everywhere," reported Dr. Gunther Rosenberg. "In a letter to the Spanish king, Charles V, he stated he counted 400 pyramids in Cholula, Mexico."

Dr. Rosenberg outlined the similarities between Egyptian and Mexican pyramids. "The sites are similar and the pyramids are oriented with great precision to those cities," he related. "Lines through their centers are of the astronomical median and the construction in grades, steps, and degrees is the same. In Egypt and Mexico, the largest pyramid is dedicated to the Sun. The Nile has a 'Valley of the Dead'; Mexico has a 'Street of the Dead.' Interior arrangements and openings are also the same. You could almost conclude the Mexicans and Egyptians used the same building plans."

In South America, rumors of treasure-laden pyramids have drawn adventurers and explorers into the isolated jungles of the Brazilian Mato Grosso. Even today, men are hunting for the lost city that caused the mysterious disappearance of Col. P. H. Fawcett's expedition in 1925. A mystic, dreamer, and explorer, Fawcett and his group simply vanished and, to date, there are only rumors about their ultimate fate.

The English explorer was seeking the City of the Caesars, said to be hidden in the interior. "The streets are paved with silver and the roofs are covered with gold," Colonel Fawcett told a newsman. "There is said to be a magical element about the place. It is visible to a few chosen seekers from the outside world. It is invisible to all undesirables. Even in modern times, explorers have disappeared hunting for the City of the Caesars."

Colonel Fawcett's last letter, sent back by runner from Dead Horse Camp in the jungles, said: "You need have no fear of failure . . ." The letter was dated May 29, 1925.

Ray Levin, a New Yorker turned treasure hunter and

soldier of fortune, spent several months hunting for Colonel Fawcett's legendary cities. "I also believe they exist," Levin declared. "Fawcett was looking for what the Indians called 'a fat tower of stones.' I think this is a pyramid. It is supposed to be capped by a 'light that never goes out.' The Indians are superstitious about the place, claiming it is haunted."

Unfortunately, Ray Levin ran out of funds. "Perhaps I'll get back there someday," he said wistfully. "There are vast ruins in the jungles that I've seen personally. But, you don't pay your way poking around in a pile of old stones."

In Wiltshire, England, Silbury Hill soars 170 feet above a five-acre base. Constructed more than 4,000 years ago, the unknown builders carried one million tons of dirt to the site. "Silbury is one of many conical mounds or stepped earthen pyramids in England," Dr. Rosenberg stated. "In Ireland, as an example, ancient graves were capped with an earthen pyramid. Early explorers in the U.S. report similar graves were found in Ohio. Pyramidal grave markers seem to have been a widespread phenomena."

France became a "land of the pyramids" with a recent discovery. "A small structure was found in the south of France, possibly built by the Knights of Templar returning from the Crusades in the 12th or 13th centuries," Dr. Rosenberg reported. "It sits over a subterranean pit, and astrological symbols are carved in the walls."

Pyramids are the greatest mystery from the ancient world. We've examined some of the sites and checked some of the rumors concerning a worldwide network of these structures. We know they were constructed in ancient times with precision and skill. We can only speculate on why and by whom they were built. Our theories would have to include:

• *They are our link with the stars!* When and if we contact beings on other planets, we're told we will communicate via mathematics. Spacemen may have left the pyramids as a mathematical code of their visits in ancient times. Their messages could be coded in the dimensions of the pyramids, or placed in a secret chamber. It would be ironic if humanity has overlooked an important message for thousands of years.

• *They are a library of ancient knowledge!* Although mankind has been on this planet for two million years, we have scant knowledge of great civilizations of the past. Faced with a disaster, such as the biblical flood, our ancestors may have hidden books, records, and histories in a secret pyramidal chamber. The Cheops pyramid alone could contain 3,700 secret depositories.

● *Pyramids are our clue to Atlantis!* Since Plato, we have sought evidence that Atlantis really existed. The pyramids may hold data on this alleged continent in the Atlantic Ocean.

● *They are what they seem to be!* The modern world has no monopoly on fads and popular phenomena. Perhaps a pyramid was simply a tomb for ancient rulers and, throughout the world, kings tried to outdo each other in building magnificent monuments. Their motto would have been, "Full speed ahead and damn the slaves!"

● *They are a source of mysterious energy!* A pyramid aligned on a north-south axis *does* create mysterious power. A Czech company sells a *cardboard* pyramid that, it claims, will resharpen a razor blade overnight. Pyramids also have a rapid dehydration effect, and an unknown "antispoilage" energy for preservation of foods. The exact nature of this energy is now being investigated.

● *They are monitoring the Earth!* The ancient astronaut theory is currently popular in both Europe and the U.S. It links biblical miracles, past catastrophes, "angels," and giant monuments to visits by starmen. Let's assume that the Earth was visited by beings from beyond the solar system. Perhaps, as some have speculated, they *seeded* homo sapiens on this planet. Or, they might want to know what's going on in the boondocks of space. They could have built a powerful intergalactic transmitter, encasing these devices inside pyramids for protection. Through the centuries, a record of earthly activities would be sent to the starmen.

Libraries . . . evidence of Atlantis . . . mathematical codes from starmen . . . intergalactic bugging devices . . . a prophecy in stone . . . whatever they are, pyramids are the most mysterious structures on our planet. It may be a decade, a score of years, or a century before science determines the answer to these puzzling enigmas.

Additional Reading

The following listing provides references to sources cited throughout this book, as well as additional, selective reading designed to supplement the reader's information from a variety of historical and contemporary viewpoints.

Bovis, Antoine, "Causerie sur le Pendule Paradiamagnétique." Nice: Au siège de l'Association des Naturalistes, Chambre de Commerce de Nice, January 28, 1931.

————"Exposé de M. A. Bovis au Congrès International de Radiotellurie à Nice, organisé par l'A.F.R.S.P. de Toulon." Undated. Contains section of "Momification par pyramide."

Davidson, David, *The Great Pyramid: Its Divine Message.* London: Williams & Norgate, 1924.

Drbal, Karel, "Les Piles Radiesthésique des MM. L. Chaumery et A. de Bélizal." Monte Carlo: Second International Congress on Psychotronic Research, 1975.

Flanagan, G. Pat, *Pyramid Power.* Santa Monica: De Vorss & Co., 1973.

————*Beyond Pyramid Power.* Santa Monica: De Vorss & Co., 1975.

Gardner, Martin, *The Incredible Dr. Matrix.* New York: Charles Scribner's, 1976.

Ostrander, Sheila, and Schroeder, Lynn, *Psychic Discoveries Behind the Iron Curtain.* Englewood Cliffs, N. J.: Prentice-Hall, 1971.

Riffert, George R. *Great Pyramid Proof of Good.* Haverhill, Mass.: Anglo-Saxon Federation of America, 1936.

Schul, Bill, and Pettit, Ed, *The Secret Power of the Pyramids.* New York: Fawcett, 1975.

Simmons, Dale, "Experiments on the Alleged Sharpening of Razor Blades and the Preservation of Flowers by Pyramids." Toronto: New York, *New Horizons,* Summer, 1973.

Smith, Warren, *The Secret Forces of the Pyramids.* New York: Zebra Books, 1975.

Taylor, John, *The Great Pyramid: Why Was It Built?* London: Longmans Green, 1863.

Tompkins, Peter, *Secrets of the Great Pyramid.* New York: Harper & Row, 1971.

Toth, Max, and Nielsen, Greg, *Pyramid Power.* New York: Freeway Press, 1974.

Valentine, Tom, *The Great Pyramid.* New York: Pinnacle Books, 1975.